HACHETTE

WINE

GUIDES

grape varieties

grape varieties

PIERRE GALET

CASSELL ILLUSTRATED

CONTENTS

Discovering...
The vine and its origins

Both wild and cultivated vines are members of the *Vitis* genus defined by the botanist Charles de Linné. They make up one of 19 genera in the *Vitaces* family. The best known variety of the *Vitis* genus, which includes all winemaking and table grapes, is *Vitis vinifera*.

Wild vines

• Vines grow wild in the temperate and warm regions of Europe, Asia, North America, Central America and Venezuela.

• Vines are now cultivated on five continents. The oldest known species of *Vitis*, which date back to the start of the Eocene period some 65 million years ago, were found in Asia (China and Japan), America (Alaska and the United States) and in France in a travertine (calcium carbonate) deposit near Sézanne in Champagne. The majority of the ancestral species, however, date back to the Miocene period (25 million years BC) when the mild climate favoured the development of the vine, even in areas where it is no longer found today. These include Iceland, Greenland, Alaska and England (although over the last two decades vinegrowing has been reintroduced successfully in England).

• Vines pre-date primitive man (who first walked on this planet some 2.5 to 3 million years BC). Many of these original vines, often known as *Labrusca*, continued to grow wild in woods throughout Europe until the arrival of phylloxera, a devastating parasite, at the end of the 19th century (see page 17). While primitive man led a nomadic life and frequently travelled in search of food, we know from the discovery of grape pips in lakeside dwellings in Switzerland and Italy that later societies were semi-nomadic or sedentary, and grew their crops close to home.

In 1606 Virginian colonial, Captain John Smith, described two types of wild vine including one with small berries that the Indians used to make juice.

Vine cultivation

- By the time of the Mesolithic period (10,000–9,000 BC) and particularly the Neolithic period (6,000–3,000 BC), man had abandoned his nomadic ways and had turned to farming. It must have been around this time, some 6,000 to 8,000 years ago, that man accidentally made a discovery that would lead to the development of an entire industry. He noticed that grapes left to stand in a pitcher would ferment spontaneously, and that the resulting liquid was mildly intoxicating. Man had discovered wine. That was the beginning of oenology and vine cultivation on an agricultural basis.
- The Würm, or final Pleistocene glaciation, led to the disappearance of many plants. A few survived in various 'climatic refuges' in Alaska, Oregon, the southeast of the United States, in the Caucasus and East Asia. Most notable among these is the 'Pontiac refuge' of the Caucasus (in Armenia, Georgia). Here, numerous plants survived thanks to the favourable climate which enjoys the moderating influence of the Caspian Sea and is shielded from the cold by the Pontic and Caucasus mountain ranges. Now regarded as one of the cradles of *Vitis vinifera* and vine cultivation, Georgia also has biblical connotations: Noah's ark is said to have come to rest on Mount Ararat, in present-day Armenia.
- The second place of historic interest, which is more or less linked to the first, was further east in Afghanistan and Kashmir from where vines brought by Asians migrating towards Europe eventually found their way southwards and westwards to the Mediterranean.
- The third centre of historic significance is thought to have been the Mediterranean Basin between Asia Minor and North Africa. Many grape varieties are known to have spread from there, thanks to the efforts of the Egyptians, the Phoenicians, the Medes, the Persians, the Greeks and the Romans. The cult of wine and the spread of viticulture is described in countless legends commemorating Osiris, Dionysus and Bacchus.
- Grape pips dating from the Bronze Age (2,000–1,000 BC) have been discovered in lakeside dwellings in Castione near Parma and on the banks of Lakes Varese, Garda and Fimon in Italy.

The spread of the vine

- Practically all cultivated vines today are the *vinifera* variety of the *Vitis* species that originated in Europe. From this primitive species, man has created a cultivable variety that has evolved considerably over the centuries, with particular regions developing their own grape varieties according to local climate and types of soil.
- In the 15th century, the conquistadores introduced *Vitis vinifera* to the American continent; in the 17th century, the Dutch planted grapes in the Cape of Good Hope; and a century later, the British started cultivating vines in Australia and New Zealand.

Pruning the vine, an 11th-century illumination from the *Homélies de Saint Grégoire de Nazianze*.

Vine species worldwide

Vitis vinifera is one of 60 varieties in the *Vitis* genus. Of these, many are infertile and others have characteristics that are unpopular with consumers, such as the 'foxy' taste and raspberry flavour typical of the American vines *Vitis labrusca*. American vines, however, are more resistant to disease than *Vitis vinifera*.

Principal American vine varieties

Labrusca aestivalis	*Vitis riparia*
Vitis berlandieri	*Vitis rupestris*
Vitis labrusca	

Principal Asian vine varieties

Vitis amurensis
Vitis coignetiae
Vitis thumbergii

Discovering...
ampelography

Cultivated vines can be distinguished by their leaves and their grapes. What *vignerons* refer to as *cépages* (**grape varieties**) and botanists know as **cultivars** are not varieties in the botanical sense of the term. They do not reproduce identical copies of themselves by means of seedlings, so propagation depends on cuttings, layering and grafting. The study of grape varieties is known as **ampelograpy**, derived from the two Greek words: *ampelos*, meaning 'vine' and *graphein*, meaning 'to write'.

The purpose of ampelography is to provide a means of identifying different grape varieties within the vineyard, wherever they are cultivated and whatever their local name. It does this by classifying the properties of each grape variety (bud burst, flowering, *véraison* or the beginning of ripening, maturity, leaf fall, yield, grape and wine quality, resistance to disease and pests, methods and training); and by describing the vine's botanical structure (leaves, shoots, inflorescence, grape bunches and individual grapes).

Cabernet Sauvignon.

Vine varieties under study are grown together in a single plot, providing an ampelographic collection on which to base long-term research of different grape varieties. Grapes harvested are vinified separately to preserve the identity of the finished wines. The botanical description of each variety is used to compile a unique identity card highlighting the characteristics that distinguish one plant from another. This can then be used to identify different vine varieties grown in a vineyard.

Detail of a
Greek vase.

Virgil and Mecene surrounded by Roman vines.

Antiquity

Latin agronomists such as Plini the Elder, Columelle, Virgil, Caton, Varron, Palladius and Isidor were interested in the properties of different vine varieties but did not describe them. In particular, they refer to grape varieties called *apianae* that attracted bees and wasps and were probably what we know today as Muscat.

Scene from a
Roman banquet.

The Middle Ages

11TH–13TH centuries

The crusaders returned home with new vines including Malvoisie, Furmint and Altesse. In a treatise on plants (*Traité des Simples*), Malaga-born Ibn-el-Baïthar (died 1248) gives details of a few vines including the Persian grape variety, Kichmich.

14TH century

In 1303 Pierre de Crescence (born Bologna 1230, died 1310) wrote *Opus ruralium commodorum*, a treatise on rural economy inspired by the ancients that describes viticulture, ampelograpy and oenology. Later, the French poet Eustache Deschamps (c. 1346–1406) was the first person to draw attention to the '*pynos de Bourgogne*', or Beaune grape variety.

13th-century
illumination of
winegrowing.

The Renaissance

16TH century

In 1513 Cardinal Ximenès commissioned Alonso de Herrera to write *Obra de agricultura, copilada de diversos autores*, a compilation on agriculture reprinted 28 times from 1520 to 1790. It includes details of various vine varieties: Torrontés, Jaén, Malvasia, Uva Palomina, Aragonés and Granaxa.

The French writer and satirist François Rabelais (1493–1550) wrote *Pantagruel* and *Gargantua* in which he refers to the vine varieties Arbois, Malvoisie, Muscadet, Breton and Chenin.

The Grape Harvest,
16th-century tapestry.

François Rabelais by
E. Delacroix.

17TH century

Andreas Baccius, Italian physician to Pope Sixte-Quinte, wrote *De Naturali vinorum historia*, a compilation of works dating back to those of ancient Latin authors.

In 1600 Olivier de Serres (1539–1619) published *Théâtre d'Agriculture*, in which he refers to many vine varieties including Pinot, Pique-Poule, Beaunois, Malvoisie, Meslier and Bourboulenc.

In 1667, in Paris, Jean Merlet published *Abrégé des Bons Fruits* giving details of several French vine varieties including Muscat Blanc de Frontignan, Raisin de Corinthe, Sauvignon Blanc, Gamet Blanc, Gamet Noir, Gouais Blanc and Gouais Violet.

Olivier de Serres.

Modern Times

18TH century

In 1736 the Chartreux monks published their *Catalogue des Chartreux*. The order was based in Paris, in the Rue de l'Enfer, and laid the initial foundations for the nursery in the Luxembourg Gardens.

In 1753 the Swedish botanist Charles de Linné published *Species plantarum* in which he describes the first species of vine known at the time: *Vitis vinifera, Vitis labrusca* and *Vitis vulpina*.

In 1780, Abbé Rozier (1734–1793) moved into Domaine de Beau-Séjour near Béziers in southern France, and established a range of ampelographic synonyms while drafting the first pages of his *Cours d'Agriculture*.

Charles de Linné.

The nursery in the Luxembourg Gardens in the 19th century.

19TH century

In 1807 Don Simón-Roxas Clemente, librarian at the Madrid botanical gardens, set to work classifying all known species of Andalusian vines. In 1817 in Italy, Count Giorgio Gallesio published *Pomona Italiana*, a study of 26 vine varieties. Three years later in Milan, Andrea Mona published *Descrizione Delle Principali Varietà di Vini*. In 1825, also in Milan, Giuseppe Acerbi published *Delle vite italiane*.

In 1841 in Austria, Franz Trummer described over 140 varieties of vine in his book *Sustematische Classification und Beschreibung der in Herzogthume Steiermark vorkommenden Rebensorten*.

In France, Count Alexandre Odart (1778–1866) published *L'Ampélographie Universelle ou Traité des Cépages les Plus Estimés*, a reference work that ran to six editions between 1845 and 1873, although it does not actually describe the vine varieties. In 1848 Hardy published his *Catalogue de l'Ecole des Vignes de la Pépinière du Luxembourg*. This collection, including 1,300 vine varieties and their synonyms, was destroyed by Baron Haussemann in the Second Empire.

Present day

The arrival of American diseases in Europe prompted various publications (most notably G. Foex in 1888, V. Puliat in 1874, 1888 and 1897, and Viala and Vermorel in 1902–1910) that focused on botanical descriptions of vine varieties so that they could be identified commercially. Thereafter, from around 1910 - 1940, there was a decline in works on ampelography. Today, at the beginning of the new millennium, ampelography uses DNA analysis to trace the lineage of each grape variety.

A bunch of Cornichon Blanc with its gherkin-shaped grapes. This table grape variety, described in the 13th century by Ibn-el-Baïthar in his *Traité des Simples* is popular throughout the Mediterranean for its curiously shaped fruit .

Grape variety names

To avoid confusion, present-day hybrids are usually known by a single name or number, in stark contrast to the elaborate names bestowed on their European ancestors. Over the centuries, vineyardists have referred to local grapes by various names based on such features as the appearance of the leaves (Pinot Meunier, because of the white 'woolly' hairs that make the leaf look as if it is dusted with flour); the shape of the grape ('Olivette' meaning a small olive, or 'Cornichon' meaning a gherkin); the advantages and disadvantages of each grape variety; their geographic origins; the name of the hybridiser, and so on. As a result, ancient European and Asian grape varieties acquired a different name each time they were introduced to a new viticultural area. As new vineyards became established worldwide, the great European grape varieties were often mistakenly called by names that bore no relation to the original plant. So we see Rhine Riesling becoming confused with Italian Riesling, and Chardonnay being confused with Chenin or Muscadet.

Understanding...
the growth cycle of the vine

Every season the vine grows by forming succulent green shoots and leaves that are the basis of the plant's development. This process, known as the **growth cycle**, starts off with bleeding (loss of sap from pruning cuts) before the buds develop, and finishes in the autumn when the vines shed their leaves.

1 Bud burst, or the emergence of the first shoots in spring.

2 The first leaves in spring.

3 Flowering.

A delicate balance

• To ensure the new season's growth, the vine must concentrate nutrients, mainly carbohydrates, in the tissues of its roots, trunk, arms and canes (which will be cut back during pruning). This anatomical change in the shoots of the vine is known as lignification.

• While the shoots are undergoing lignification, sugars are transferred towards the grapes, and growth substances are laid down in the seeds to ensure the development of future generations.

• The key to good vine management lies in maintaining this delicate balance between the concentration of the nutrients in the growing points needed to ensure next year's growth, and the translocation of sugars essential for nourishing the grapes and seeds. The vineyardist must maintain this balance so as not to compromise the life expectancy of the vine.

4. Inflorescence (flower buds) in the early stages of the growth cycle.

5 *Véraison*, or first colour: the grapes start to change colour and sugar concentration increases at about the same rate as acidity decreases.

6 Maturity: grapes are at peak maturity when acidity is no longer falling and sugar concentrations have stabilised.

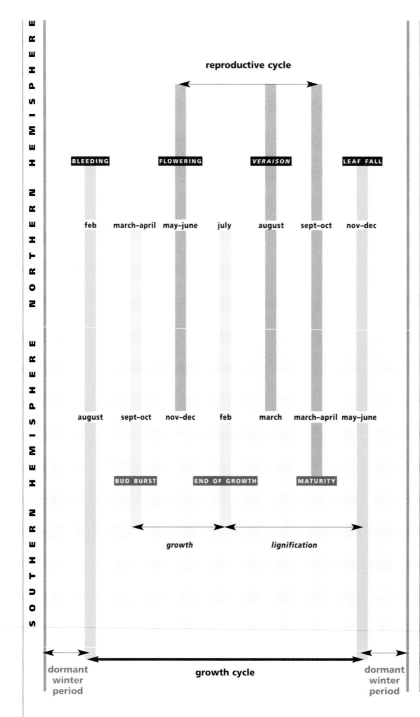

NORTHERN HEMISPHERE

SOUTHERN HEMISPHERE

reproductive cycle

BLEEDING		FLOWERING		VERAISON		LEAF FALL
feb	march–april	may–june	july	august	sept–oct	nov–dec
august	sept–oct	nov–dec	feb	march	march–april	may–june
	BUD BURST		END OF GROWTH		MATURITY	

growth   lignification

dormant
winter
period

growth cycle

dormant
winter
period

The vine in temperate climates

• In temperate climates, the vine grows in an interrupted fashion, periods of growth (active life) alternating with periods of rest (dormant life).

• In northern hemispheres, **bud burst**, when the first shoots appear, occurs in early spring (March to April), marking a return to visible signs of life. It is often preceded by bleeding, also in early spring, when sap starts to weep from pruning wounds.

• April to late July or early August is the growth period when the shoots grow long and leafy. The leaves play an essential role in the absorption of the chlorophyll that transforms crude sap into complex sap, and in ensuring gaseous interchange through respiration and transpiration. In late July to early August, depending on the climate and the grape variety, shoots stop growing as the vine starts to lignify, concentrating nutrients in the shoots that now harden and turn brown. These anatomical changes in the vine continue into October.

• During the autumn, the leaves gradually cease functioning, turn yellow and eventually fall from the canes: their cells are no longer able to absorb chlorophyll, which now disappears. **Leaf fall** marks the end of the growth cycle and the start of the winter **dormant** period.

• The vine's reproductive cycle involves the formation,

development and fertilisation of inflorescences (flower buds), followed by the growth of clusters of baby grapes, which develop into ripe fruit and seeds. A few days after bud burst, the first tiny inflorescences emerge from the growing tips and continue growing until the **flowering** period (15 May to end June in the south of France and until July in northern regions). Only 30 per cent of the flowers are pollinated and develop into grapes during a process known as **setting**. Subsequent poor weather conditions can interfere with fruitage. *Véraison* (**first colour**) or the beginning of ripening when the grapes start to change colour also depends on the geographical area: from mid-July onwards for early-ripening varieties in the south of France, to early August in other parts of the country. In northern vineyards the grapes continue to change colour until September.

• **Harvesting** depends on the type of grape (whether table or wine grape) and the location of the vineyard. The harvesting of early-ripening table grapes may begin in late July in France, late June in Spain, Italy, Greece and North Africa or even late May in Israel. The harvesting of early-ripening wine grapes, such as Chardonnay, may begin in the second half of August in the south of France and continue into October throughout the rest of the country. In Alsace, pickers can still be harvesting *vendanges tardives* (late-harvest)

grapes and *grains nobles* (grapes that have been botrytised by the fungus *Botrytis cinerea*, otherwise known as noble rot) in November.

• In the southern hemisphere, where the seasons are reversed, bud burst occurs from September to October, flowering takes place in November and the growth season lasts until February. Depending on the vine varieties and the topographical location of the vineyard, harvesting usually starts between February and mid-May. The vines then lose their leaves and remain dormant until September.

The vine in tropical climates

• In tropical climates, where the growth cycle is never interrupted by falls in temperature below 12°C/54°F, the vine grows and fruits continuously. In principle, therefore, vineyards in tropical countries should yield three crops of grapes per year, but in practice the grapes vary in quality and usually the only commercially viable crop is harvested during the dry or less rainy season.

• In the northern hemisphere, the closer you get to the equator, the earlier bud burst occurs. As a result, provided the vines are pruned twice a year, they will produce two crops of grapes, except in vineyards planted at altitude where they only fruit once a year. Vines that fruit twice yearly flower briefly two weeks after pruning.

• In the southern hemisphere,

however, there can be one or two grape harvests depending on the altitude of the vineyard and the duration of the rainy season. In Java, for instance, there is no dormant period. Vines grow and fruit continuously, with different plants displaying bunches of grapes at different stages of their development, from flowering inflorescences to ripe bunches of grapes ready for picking.

Vigour
Plant vigour is an indicator of the metabolic rate of its growth organs as demonstrated, in particular, by its rate of respiration, synthesis of organic compounds through photosynthesis and speed of growth. Vigour in a vine is measurable by the weight of the pruned wood. It depends not only on climate, soil, stock and grape variety, but also on the conditions of cultivation: density of planting, training methods, soil maintenance, irrigation, fertiliser and preventative treatments used.

Understanding...
diseases that affect the vine

The vine is at the mercy of an army of diseases and insects that demand constant vigilance on the part of the *vignerons* to ensure a healthy harvest and quality wines. They must also, however, safeguard the ecosystem by using environmentally friendly methods wherever possible.

Fungal infections

In the 19th century, viticulture in Europe was devastated by three major fungal infections imported from the United States: downy mildew, powdery mildew (oidium) and black rot. Their arrival marked the end of genuinely 'organic' methods of cultivation, free of all chemical additives of mineral (copper, sulphur) or organic origin. In 1885 Alexis Millardet, professor of botany at the University of Bordeaux, and Ulysse Gayon, director of the Oenology Centre of Bordeaux, studied the effects of Bordeaux mixture, a fungicide

Powdery mildew (oidium).

prepared by mixing solutions of copper and slaked lime.

• **Downy mildew** (*Plasmopara viticola*) invades the leaves and clusters coating the inner surface with a white powdery substance. An attack of downy mildew can wipe out an entire harvest.

• **Powdery mildew or oidium** (*Uncinula necator*) feeds off the sap and attacks the surface of the green parts of the vine, which become coated with grey dust. It also damages the grapes, increasing their vulnerability to grey rot.

• **Black rot** (*Guignardia bidwellii*), the third of the American diseases,

Anthracnose (black spot).

Grey rot.

Downy mildew.

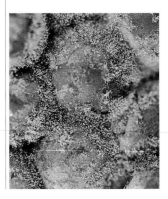

Leaf roll (left).

The life-cycle of
phylloxera (right).

covers the leaves with little blotches
followed by black pustules. The
grapes become totally dehydrated
and also develop pustules.

• Another death-dealing fungus
is **anthracnose** (*gloesporium
ampelophagum*) also known as
'black spot'. It affects the leaves
which become covered in little
blotches, then holes, leaving a coal
black border.

• Wet autumns create ideal
conditions for **grey rot** (*Botryotinia
fuckeliana* formerly known as
Botrytis cinerea). This mainly attacks
the bunches of grapes.

• Finally there are **apoplexy** or
esca ('black measles'), **eutypiose**
(*Eutypa lata*) and **root rot** or **oak
root fungus** (*Rosellinia necatrix*
and *Armirallariella mellea*). These all
attack the wood, entering the trunk
through pruning wounds and
gradually killing the root. After
pruning, therefore, the vineyardist
must disinfect the pruning woods
and destroy all dead wood.

Viral diseases

In Europe, **court-noué**, or
infectious degeneration of the vine,
is a fairly common cause of crop
failure. Affected vines are
characterised by dwarfing of shoots
and leaves and *coulure* (non-setting
of fruit) on early-season growth.
Other viral diseases include **leaf roll**
and **bark virus**.

Parasites

• **Phylloxera** (*Dactylosphaera
vitifollii*) was imported from the
United States in the 19th century
and destroyed the majority of
European vineyards which had to
be replanted with resiliant stock.
This tiny, hermaphroditic root louse
has a complex life-cycle living both
underground on the roots, and
above ground on the leaves and
green parts of the vine. Its most
devastating effect, however, is
below ground, where it sucks the
life out of the roots, killing the
stock.

17

• **Grape moth larvae** usually refer to the larvae of the tortrix and grape berry moths that attack the flower buds and grapes. For some years now, French vineyards have also come under attack from the western grape root worm. Finally, there is the vine pyralid caterpillar that attacks not only the grapes but also the leaves.

Grape moth pupa.

Grape moth larva.

Grape moth imago.

• **Scale insects** cause severe damage by exuding a honeyed syrup onto the leaves and grapes which encourages the development of a fungal disease called sooty mould. The affected parts of the vine turn black and table grapes become unsaleable.

• **Coleoptera** of various forms are another pest although attacks can now be brought under control. They include the larvae of the long-horned beetle (*Vesperus xatarti*) found in vineyards in the Roussillon (Banyuls and Rivesaltes) and the Aude (Fitou) in France.

• **Leafhoppers** are biting insects whose larvae feed off the wood of the vine. The adults live on the underside of the leaf, biting into the veins to suck out the sap. Some species are known to spread infections such as Pierce's disease.

• **Eelworms** (Nematodes) are small worms that attack the roots, either invading the tissues or living off the exterior. They may also transmit viral diseases. Some of these worms live for several years and

Benoît Raclet conquers the vine pyralid caterpillar

The Beaujolais region in France used to be plagued by pyralid caterpillars. Then in 1827, a *vigneron* called Benoît Raclet from the village of Romanèche made a chance discovery. He noticed that the vines growing outside his kitchen window, which were regularly doused with hot water, remained lush and green. This led him to scald all his vines in a bid to destroy the pyralid caterpillars hiding in the bark. His discovery, however, was greeted with such derision that Raclet abandoned his research. When he returned to it 10 years later, pyralid caterpillars had wreaked so much havoc that Raclet's method seemed the only solution. From 1843, scalding the vines became standard practice. Today Raclet's bust stands in the Place de Romanèche and every year on the last Sunday in October *vignerons* drink his health during the festival of the new Beaujolais and Mâconnais wines.

one species in particular, *Xiphinema*, can go without food for long periods, thus surviving to contaminate the new crop when the time is particularly short between two harvests.

• **Grape rust mites**, including yellow spiders (*Eotetranychus carpini*) and red spiders (*Panonychus ulmi*), are no newcomers to the vineyard and caused little damage until relatively recently, thanks to a balanced ecosystem. In 1950, however, that balance was disturbed by the use of insecticides based on phosphoric and carbamate esters. Summer infestations can interfere with photosynthesis, preventing the grapes from maturing properly and jeopardising both the quality of the harvest and the future wine.

Red spiders.

In New Zealand, vine growers drape the grapes in netting to protect them from the unwanted attentions of birds (Martinborough, North Island).

Animals

The vine is also preyed on by a variety of animals that enjoy eating both the grapes and the leaves. Birds peck away at the grapes, thus damaging the fruit and exposing it to attacks of rot – starlings are particularly fond of grapes and regularly pillage the vineyard. Birds, as well as bees and wasps, go after the sugar in the grapes, especially the sweetness of Muscat grapes, so much so indeed that in Roman times Muscat grapes became known as *uva apianae* or 'bee grapes'.

Environmentally friendly methods of vineyard protection

Bordeaux mixture, fumigation, routine chemical treatments: these were just some of the methods used by *vignerons* in their struggle to combat the pests and parasites that had devastated the vineyards in the early 20th century. While the end may have been justified, the means had serious consequences for the environment and the vine itself. Insects learned to adapt to the new treatments and future generations became resistant to them. All around the vineyards, the water and soil often became polluted by toxic waste, destroying the wildlife essential to maintaining a balanced soil, not to mention the small concentrations of toxic residues that were also present in the grapes and the finished wine. The phytopharmaceutical products available today are specially designed to be effective at lower doses.

Understanding...
cultivation to produce premium wines

All vineyards of the world, whether newly established or replanted, now grow the great French noble grape varieties. These include Cabernet Sauvignon, Pinot Noir, Chardonnay, Sauvignon, Syrah and others. The fashion for *vins de cépage* (wines made from one grape variety rather than a blend) partly accounts for this trend. But while varieties can be exported to other countries, the quality of the final wines produced is influenced by an extra, most important factor: the *terroir*.

The effect of *terroir*

Terroir refers to the complete growing environment: a combination of natural factors including altitude, aspect, climate, soil type and topography that influence the characteristics of grape varieties and the wines produced. Vines are cultivated in many different types of terrain but they prefer thin, well-drained soils that limit the yields. Vineyards planted on well-exposed slopes are especially favoured as they encourage maturation but prevent water from stagnating at the foot of the plants. Vineyards planted on low-lying ground, though, are usually used for the production of large volumes of lower-quality wine.

While France has always attached particular importance to the role of *terroir*, winemakers in other countries viewed the concept differently, some setting greater store by quality of the grape variety and vinification techniques.

Newcomers to the world of viticulture, however, have learned not to underestimate *terroir*. How else are we to account for the spectacular results achieved in some areas of the Napa Valley in California, or in red limestone regions of the *terra rosa* in Coonawarra, Australia? It is the task of the vineyardist to bring out the characteristic qualities of the grapes from the growing environment.

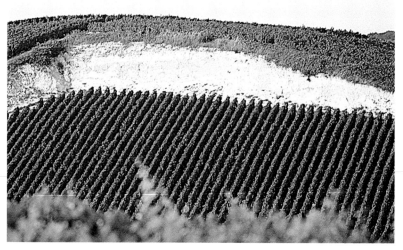

Vineyards in Chablis: these marly soils are well-suited to the Chardonnay grape.

Density of planting

Density of planting, or the number of vines per hectare, is a decisive factor in the quality of the wine produced. Formerly, French vineyards were very densely planted, with the number of vines per hectare ranging from 10,000 in Bordeaux to 50,000 in Champagne. With so little soil, individual plants tended to be weak with just a few good bunches of grapes. Following replanting of the vineyards after the phylloxera epidemic, the space between the rows of vines has been widened to allow machinery to circulate. That said, the density of planting in quality vineyards still stands at around 10,000 vines per hectare.

Left: chalky soils, such as those on the Côte des Blancs in the Champagne region, provide a regular, moderate supply of water and encourage deep-rooted vines.

Extreme weather conditions, such as flooding after torrential rain or sub-zero temperatures, are disastrous for the health of the vineyard and the future harvest.

Winter pruning determines the volume of future production.

'The genius of wine lies in the grape variety' wrote Olivier de Serres at the start of the 17th century. Today's *vigneron* knows that the role of *terroir* is just as important.

Training and pruning

Vines may be trained or untrained according to how they are pruned. Vines grown untrained are short-pruned (methods known as bush and goblet pruning). Trained vines are attached to trellises or other supports (Royat cordon and Guyot pruning methods). The method of pruning determines the number of grape bunches borne by each plant. A reasonable number of bunches ensures that the grapes tend to

Manual grape harvesting at Château Latour in Pauillac, Bordeaux.

After pruning, the cut wood is burnt or turned into chippings and mixed into the soil.

ripen more easily and concentrate their aromas. Pruning therefore affects both quantity and quality. Other factors that play a part in determining the quantity or quality of output of grapes are tying-back, irrigation, manuring, 'green harvests' (to remove surplus grape bunches early on), tilling, clearing the grass or grassing over.

Cloning

All plants that are propagated from the original vinestock, whether by grafts or by cuttings, are its descendants or clones. The majority of European vine varieties grown are the product of clonal selection with such similar characteristics that for a long time they were known under the same name. Over the centuries, however, vine growers learned to distinguish between different clones and to give each one a separate name based on the name of the original creator (Pinot Liébault, for example) or the place or origin (such as Pinot de Pernand). Clones may be distinguished by the shape of the leaf, which may be more or less serrated and villous (covered in hairs), or by their growing habits (early ripening, volume of production, resistance to disease etc.). Clonal selection in France today is very advanced and has become carefully supervised by an organisation set up to be responsible for ensuring the quality of clones: the Établissement National Technique pour

l'Amélioration de la Viticulture (ENTAV). Based in Grau-du-Roi in the Gard, the ENTAV collects clones and assesses their performance before releasing them to nurseries and resale to viticulturalists.

New grape varieties

New varieties of grape may occur naturally as a result of sudden changes in plant characteristics through mutation. However, ever since primitive man first started to pick wild grapes, he has looked for ways to increase yields, improve the quality of grapes and eradicate diseased plants. The phylloxera crisis prompted *vignerons* and scientists to explore the possibilities of hybridisation in a bid to separate the advantages of parent plants from their disadvantages. Genetic research, as it is now known, led to the development of new disease-resistant vine varieties called 'hybrid direct producers', and pest-resistant vine varieties for use as rootstock. In fact, ever since the phylloxera crisis at the end of the 19th century, most grape varieties must be grafted onto the disease-resistant root system of another vine (the rootstock). Ungrafted vines are now limited to a handful of vineyards such as those planted in sandy soils where there is little risk of phylloxera, and vineyards that are regularly flooded, such as those situated in the Camargue region of southern France.
Today, genetic engineering is used in molecular biology to introduce

genes that carry the codes for beneficial effects (such as disease resistance). They may be introduced into the chromosomes of vulnerable vines, or incorporated into the genotypes of rootstock. The current boom in molecular biology is reflected by the development of GMOs (genetically modified organisms) that initially require more exhaustive safety testing before they can be reproduced on a commercial basis. Other techniques used to improve vines include *in vitro* cultivation of micro cuttings taken from isolated organs.

Vin de cépage or vin d'assemblage

A *vin de cépage* is a wine made from one particular grape and is known as a single varietal wine; a *vin d'assemblage* is a blended wine made from several varieties. Two of the most popular single varietal wines produced today are Cabernet Sauvignon (red wine) and Chardonnay (white). Blended wine is produced from a combination of complementary grape varieties such as Merlot and Cabernet Sauvignon in the case of Bordeaux.

Identifying...
the vine

In their wild state, vines are vigorous climbers. They grow by putting out runners that attach themselves wherever they can by their tendrils to reach the tops of trees and walls, and to expose their foliage to the sunlight. Cultivated vines, by contrast, grow relatively little because of annual pruning. Certain strains, however, are prodigious growers capable of spreading over large areas and producing several hundred kilograms of grapes. Examples include the trellised Chasselas vine in Fontainebleu near Paris and the vine at Hampton Court (Black Hamburgh) on the outskirts of London. The trunks of such vines can measure more than a metre in circumference.

The growing tip

The growing tip is formed by the buds that ensure the vine's survival from one year to the next. They produce shoots, leaves and inflorescences that in turn produce new buds. One of the keys to identifying different grape varieties are the **villous** (soft, woolly hairs) on the surface of the growing tip. According to density of growth, these are described by ampelographers as *felty* (if tightly packed and entirely covering the leaf), *downy* (if less dense, revealing the green colour of the leaf beneath) or *cobwebby* (if thinly spread like a cobweb).

Grenache vine with downy growing tip.

Riparia Gloire vine with glabrous (hairless) growing tips.

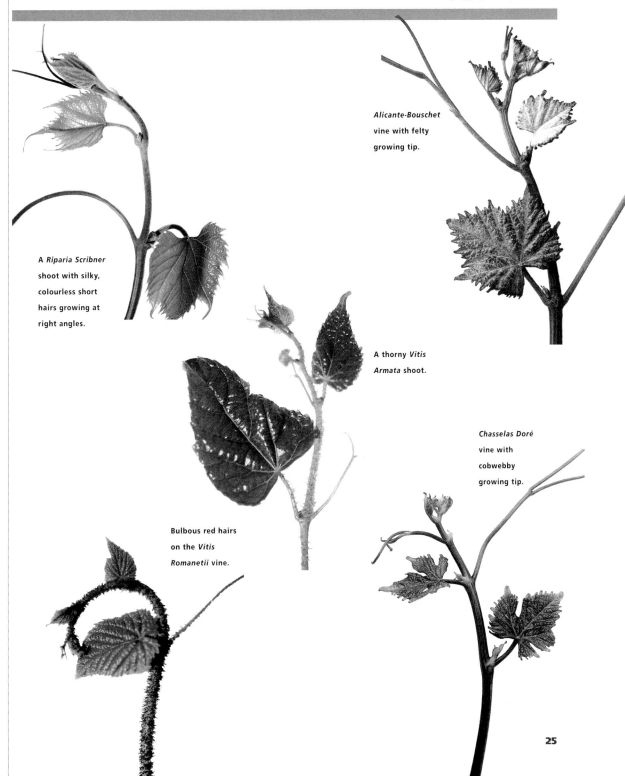

Alicante-Bouschet vine with felty growing tip.

A *Riparia Scribner* shoot with silky, colourless short hairs growing at right angles.

A thorny *Vitis Armata* shoot.

Chasselas Doré vine with cobwebby growing tip.

Bulbous red hairs on the *Vitis Romanetii* vine.

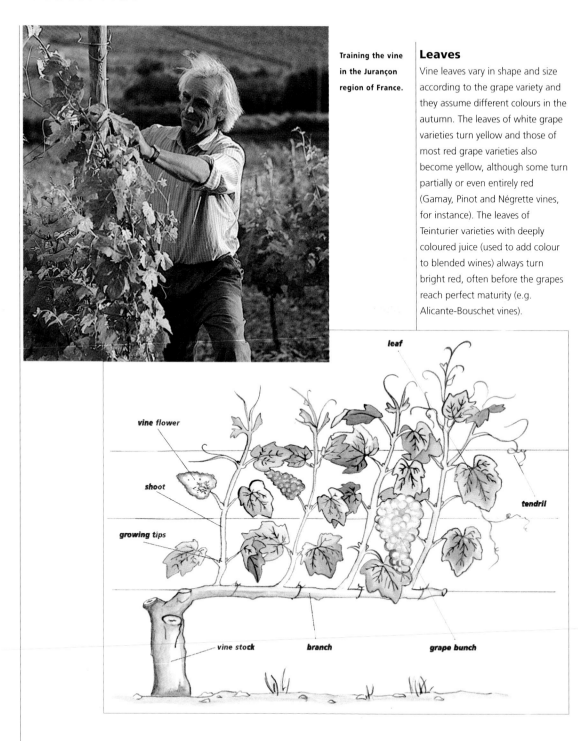

Training the vine in the Jurançon region of France.

Leaves

Vine leaves vary in shape and size according to the grape variety and they assume different colours in the autumn. The leaves of white grape varieties turn yellow and those of most red grape varieties also become yellow, although some turn partially or even entirely red (Gamay, Pinot and Négrette vines, for instance). The leaves of Teinturier varieties with deeply coloured juice (used to add colour to blended wines) always turn bright red, often before the grapes reach perfect maturity (e.g. Alicante-Bouschet vines).

leaf

vine flower

shoot

growing tips

tendril

vine stock

branch

grape bunch

Shoots

Every year, the growing tips produce shoots up to several metres long. Each shoot is composed of a stem that is swollen at intervals (called nodes). Nodes give rise to various growth organs: leaves that attach by the stalk and grow from alternate nodes; buds that form in the pit of the stalk; laterals or small shoots that are usually infertile but occasionally produce grapes; and finally tendrils that grow on the side of the node opposite the leaves. Except for a few vines whose shoots are distinguished by their woolly villosity, most shoots look similar. With some varieties, however, the colour of the bark provides a useful clue as to the type of vine: straw yellow in the case of Grenache; light beige richly coated with purple bloom in the case of Cinsaut.

Flowers

Flowers bloom in spring as soon as the buds appear. They are always opposite the leaves and present as clusters of corollas, each composed of five joined petals that detach at the base during flowering. These little inflorescences are small and usually light yellow in colour, although those of Teinturier vines and some American species are red to bright red. Most cultivated vines are hermaphrodites. Inflorescences vary in size from 4 cm (1.5 inches) for wild vines to more than 50 cm (19.6 inches)

The long shoots of the Palestine grape.

for some table grapes (particularly Palestine grapes). The size of the blossoms influences the size of the grape bunches.

Grape bunches

The number of bunches depends on the successful flowering and proper setting of the fruit (grape development following pollination). The shape of the bunch varies with each variety.

27

Identifying...
the leaves

Leaves are present throughout the growth cycle of the vine and are easily kept in a herbarium for research and comparison. They are the principal key to identifying a grape variety.

The leaves of cultivated vines are almost always single, palmate, with five main veins coming from the petiole that form the branches of the leaf blade. The differences in the leaf shapes illustrated below are due to variations in the length of the main veins, and to differences in the length of the lateral veins in relation to the middle vein, and in the angles formed between them. This is known as the science of **ampelometry** and it confirms common leaf shapes on the basis of precise leaf measurements.

The **dentations** of the leaf blade are important when examining vines. Some vine leaves have no indentations at all. Others on the contrary are *lacinate* or shaped like a parsley leaf (such as the leaves of the Chasselas Cioutat variety). Vine leaves are usually five-lobed but some are trilobate (three lobes) and others are entire (unlobed). Certain vine varieties have leaves with more than five lobes (ranging from seven to nine).

Lacinate leaf of the Chasselas Cioutat vine.

Clarette vine leaf showing petiolar sinus with overlapping lobes.

Lateral sinuses are particularly interesting in shape. These tend to from a V-shaped sinus to a concave sinus, with open or overlapping lobes.

The opening of the **petiolar sinus** is another identifying factor to consider. The petiolar sinus may be narrow or closed with overlapping lobes (such as the leaf of the Clairette vine shown opposite) or shaped like an accolade and 'naked' (such as the leaves of the Chardonnay and Cabernet Sauvignon vines which are both illustrated below).

Although the **general aspect** of the leaf blade is a secondary characteristic it can sometimes modify the appearance of foliage in a characteristic manner. A leaf may be described in the following ways: *smooth* when the surface of the blade is smooth; *bullate* when 'bubbles' are visible between the smaller vein subdivisions; *crimped* when the bulges are at least 1 cm (0.3 inches) in diameter and form hollows and large dents; and *wavy* when the bulges are visible between and parallel to the main veins. While the upper surface of a blade is usually completely hairless (except in the case of Pinot Meunier), the hairiness of the underside is closely related to the villosity of the growing tip.

The **leaf contour** completes our description of vine foliage. A leaf is described as flat if the entire blade remains on the same plane; *en goutière* if it is folded along the central vein; *contorted* if the blade is deeply undulating so that it will not lie flat in a herbarium (as with Grenache); involute when the leaf turns up into a cup shape so that the upperside is entirely hidden by the underside; *revolute* when the leaf turns down at the edges revealing only the upperside of the blade and often concealing the 'teeth' (as with the Alicante-Bouschet and Muscadet varieties).

Dentation provides an excellent visual ampelographic characteristic. The teeth on the margins of a leaf vary widely. These can be practically non-existent but may also be wide, large or more or less narrow.

Chardonnay (left) and Cabernet Sauvignon (right) vine leaves have a 'naked' petiolar sinus.

shape	description	examples

Reniform

The leaf is wider than it is long; the sum of its angles is less than 130°

Rupestris (Lot *département*), 110 Richter (1), 1103 Paulsen

Orbicular

Rounded leaf

Clarette, Cinsaut, Chenin, Ugni Blanc, Aligoté (2), Gewürztraminer (3)

Cuneiform (wedge-shaped)

The leaf is in effect composed of a square and a triangle

Vitis riparia and *Berlandieri-riparia* (161–49C) (4), *Vitis Embergeri* (5 and 9)

Truncate

Orbicular leaf with shortened L_3 vein

Vitis aestivalis, Mauzac, *Vitis pentagona* (6), *Vitis Lincecumii* (7)

Cordiform

Heart-shaped leaf (probably the most archetypal leaf shape)

Asian vine varieties *Vitis armata*, *betulifolia, flexuosa, Romanetii* (8), the American variety *Vitis cordifolia*

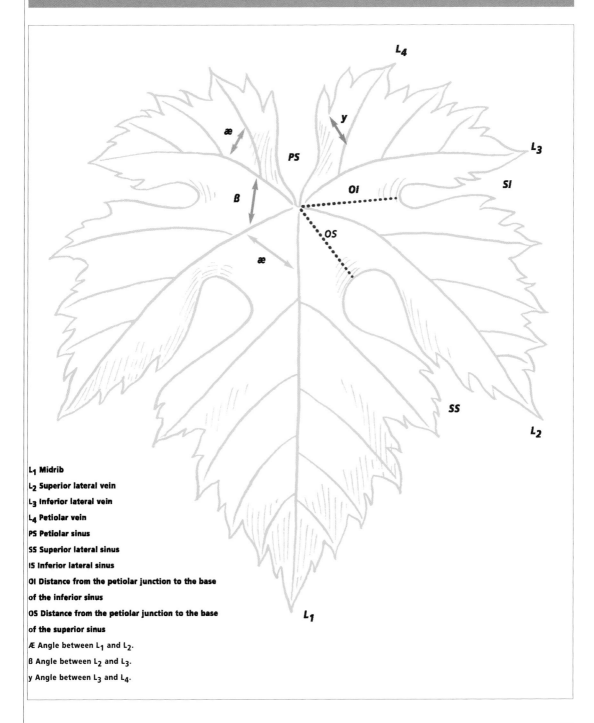

L₁ **Midrib**
L₂ **Superior lateral vein**
L₃ **Inferior lateral vein**
L₄ **Petiolar vein**
PS Petiolar sinus
SS Superior lateral sinus
IS Inferior lateral sinus
OI Distance from the petiolar junction to the base
of the inferior sinus
OS Distance from the petiolar junction to the base
of the superior sinus
Æ Angle between L₁ and L₂.
ß Angle between L₂ and L₃.
y Angle between L₃ and L₄.

Identifying...
the grape bunches

Because of their commercial value, grape bunches have always been studied by ampelographers in a bid to establish a set of classifications based on the shape and colour of the fruit. In reality, bunches are a secondary characteristic that is observable for a few days only as the grapes reach maturity.

Large and small

The size of the bunch of grapes is certainly a distinctive characteristic and ranges from large to small depending on the variety of grape grown. However, variations in size are also observable within a single grape variety depending on the fertility of the soil, manuring, irrigation and vine management (planting density, the system of pruning and potential crop) and chemical treatments (growth regulators, for instance). The very small bunches found on wild vines measure less than 6 cm (2.3 inches) in length and weigh less than 50 grams (1.76 oz). Compare this with very large bunches measuring more than 24 cm (9.5 inches) in length and weighing more than a kilo (2.2 lb).

Assorted shapes

Grape bunches can be either cylindrical or truncate in shape depending on the number and length of the lateral branches of the bunch's stem. The first secondary lateral branch (the one nearest to the peduncle) may grow and separate off from the rest of the bunch forming a 'wing'. Some vine varieties, such as Sultanine, have bunches with several wings. Occasionally these grow to be the same size as the principal bunch making it look like a double. The density of the bunches is determined by the space inbetween the grapes. Bunches are described as *loose* when the grapes are visibly separate from each other. This is an advantage in the case of table grapes these should be easy to pull away from the vine with the fingers. Conversely, bunches are *compact* when the grapes are pressed together and are much more difficult to detach, giving the bunch a pine cone, or sausage-like appearance.

The Grapes

Grapes are the edible part of the bunch and are measured by diameter, volume and weight.

Type of grape	Diameter	Volume (per 100 grapes)	Weight (per 100 grapes)
Very small	< 8 mm (0.3 in)	< 30 cm^3 (12 in^3)	< 35 g (1.2 oz)
Small	8–12 mm (0.31–0.47 in)	31–100 cm^3 (12–39 in^3)	36–110 g (1.2–2.8 oz)
Medium	12–18 mm (0.46–0.70 in)	101–300 cm^3 (40–118 in^3)	111–330 g (3.8–11.5 oz)
Large	18–24 mm (0.70–0.93 in)	301–650 cm^3 (118–255 in^3)	331–700 g (11.5–24.5 oz)
Very large	> 24 mm (0.93 in)	> 650 cm^3 (255 in^3)	> 700 g (24.5 oz)

The shape of the grapes helps us to distinguish between the different varieties. The simplest, most common shape is almost spherical but there are many variations on this. Grapes that are more or less flat at each end are described as *discoid* or disc-shaped (these are found on wild vines). Those that are flatter longitudinally range from *ellipsoid* (shaped like a rugby ball) to *fusiform* (more strongly tapered). Egg-shaped grapes that are flatter at the base than at the top are described as *ovoid* (egg-shaped), or *obovoid* if narrower at the top. There are also cylindroidal grapes which when elongated become more like a date. Finally there are grapes that look like a cone with the point cut off (*ovoid-truncate*) and those with varying numbers of bumps or depressions, which are described as *arched*.

Grape shape is only really important for table grapes: bunches of ellipsoid grapes (Dattier, Italia, for example) are considered more attractive. In the Middle East consumers tend to prefer grapes that are arched, date-shaped, fusiform or ovoid-truncate.

Grape **colour** is an important distinguishing feature and can vary from green to a very dark blue-black. Colour is due to the presence of anthocyanins: a group of colouring pigments that, depending on the species or variety of grape, can vary in number from three to 18. The colour of the grapes depends on the nature of those anthocyanins and their relative proportions. Pink grape varieties, for instance, contain just three to six anthocyanins, whereas red varieties contain 13–18. Teinturier varieties with coloured flesh have different types of anthocyanin in the flesh than in the skin. White grape varieties contain no anthocyanins at all, except occasionally when overripe (as can be seen with Admirable de Courtiller varieties). Nor do white grapes contain more flavonols (yellow pigments) than the coloured varieties.

Taste is a critical factor in the production of both table and wine grapes. Many grape varieties have a rather neutral taste, resembling slightly acidic, sweetened water, while others have more distinctive flavours, some of which are popular (musk and orange blossom, for example), some of which are not (the grassy taste of wild vines, the bitter taste of *Vitis cordifolia*). Some varieties are popular in the USA but not in Europe (the 'foxy' or raspberry taste of *Vitis labrusca,* for example).

Grape **seeds** are usually pear-shaped with a pointed 'beak' that may be more or less pronounced. Grape varieties that do not produce seeds are known as *seedless*.

Grape colour

In principle, every grape variety should produce bunches in the full range of colours: white, black and the deep red of the Teinturier varieties. This principle applies to all cultivated grape varieties that have remained in their region of origin where they evolved from the spontaneous form of *Vitis silvestris*. In Burgundy, for instance, Pinot Noir vines have long produced grapes in a variety of colours that are specially selected by growers. In addition to Pinot Noir, there are Pinot Teinturier, Pinot Tête de Nègre, Pinot Rouge, Pinot Rose or Pinot Mongeard, Pinot Gris, Pinot Blanc and even Pinot Cioutat vines with parsley-shaped leaves. In the south of France, a grape variety such as Terret can produce plants with one branch bearing red grapes, the second one bearing grey grapes and the third one consisting of white grapes. Carignan, Grenache and Aramon also produce grapes in three basic colours (red, pink or grey, and white). It seems likely, therefore, that French grape varieties which produce bunches of a single colour originated abroad. The other colours remained in the country of origin or were completely wiped out during the phylloxera epidemic, or earlier still by wars and religious turmoil and upheaval.

Identifying aromas

Gas chromatography is used to create a graphic 'aromagramme' which can analyse the volatile constituents of aroma in grapes. In this process for identifying aromas inert gas circulates in a tube serving as a vehicle for volatile molecules. As the gas leaves the tube, the mass of each molecule is plotted on a curve as a series of peaks. More than 500 constituents may be identified in this way, some in very low concentrations.

Dense, cylindrical bunch of Pinot Noir.

Loose bunch of Muscat de Hambourg.

Fairly loose, conical bunch of Dattier de Beyrouth.

Cylindrical bunch of Baroque grapes with a small wing.

The cellars of Château Dillon in Haut-Médoc, Bordeaux.

Winged,
cylindrical-conical
bunch of
Carignan.

Loose, truncate
bunch of Aligoté.

Winged, conical
bunch of
Tibouren.

Cylindrical-conical
bunch of Italia.

Fairly loose,
truncate
bunch of
Gewürztraminer.

Loose cylindrical
bunch of
La Reine des
Vignes.

Winged,
truncate bunch
of Gamay-Fréaux.

Dense,
cylindrical-conical
bunch of
Sylvaner.

Aligoté

This Burgundian grape could have easily disappeared. *Vignerons* on the Côte d'Or and the Côte Chalonnaise tended to prefer the region's Chardonnay. Yet today Aligoté is highly regarded. Indeed it was authorised in 1938 for the production of Charlemagne Grand Cru, one of Burgundy's finest white wines.

Bouzeron

Bouzeron in the Côte Chalonnaise, north of the *département* of Saône-et-Loire, is planted with 65 hectares of Aligoté vines grown on marl and limestone soils at an altitude of 150–300 metres (492–984 ft). Bouzeron is a dry white wine in shades of pale gold with light green highlights. The aroma has marked fragrances of acacia and hazelnut, punctuated by mineral notes. Blended with discreet quantities of Chardonnay, Bouzeron Aligoté wines acquire a pleasing roundness that tempers their natural vivacity.

Vineyard profile

Aligoté is a vigorous grape variety characterised by early bud burst. It does particularly well on slopes, regularly producing 50–70 hectolitres of wine per hectare. Output from Romanian vineyards is three times this amount.

In France

Aligoté has made continuous progress and currently covers more than 1,700 hectares of French vineyards. It is planted in the *départements* of the Jura and Savoie, as well as in the valley of the Drôme, where it shares the Châtillon-en-Diois appellation alongside Chardonnay. Aligoté started life on the slopes of Burgundy before retreating to the plains when Chardonnay became more fashionable. Today it is

Identifying the grape variety

Aligoté has a downy white growing tip. The leaves are medium sized, trilobate but so poorly defined as to appear entire. Leaf margins are sharply serrated with slightly revolute edges. The blade's underside of is cobwebby-pubescent with a lyre-shaped petiolar sinus. Grape bunches are small, cylindrical or truncate and the grapes are small, spherical and orange-white.

honoured as one of the only grape varieties to lend its name to a Burgundian appellation: Bourgogne-Aligoté. In 1997, Aligoté was confirmed as one of the great wines when it was granted its own communal appellation status under the Bouzeron denomination. Aligoté contributes to the production of Crémant-de-Bourgogne.

Around the world

Aligoté travels well and is planted in vineyards throughout the countries of the former USSR (Moldavia, the Ukraine, Georgia, Azerbaijan and even Kazakhstan) and in many east European countries. In Romania the grapes are picked when overripe to produce wines with low acidity. Aligoté can also be used to make sparkling wines. In Bulgaria, in the southern region of Chirpan, Aligoté adds liveliness to blended premium

Also known as ...

Griset Blanc in Beaune, Plant Gris around Meursault, Plant de Trois Raisins to the north of Dijon, Blanc de Troyes in Gevrey, Troyen Blanc and Chaudenet Gras on the Côte Chalonnaise and Vert Blanc in the Jura.

dry white wines for the export market. It is also planted in Switzerland, Canada and California, and in Chile, where it is blended with Sémillon and Riesling. Cultivation of Aligoté worldwide is in the region of 23,000 hectares.

Colour and Taste

Aligoté is a crisp, light white wine for drinking young. It is most famous as an aperitif mixed with crème de Cassis, otherwise known as a 'Kir' after the Canon and deputy mayor of Dijon who first made the mixture famous in 1945. To think of Aligoté in these terms only would be to do it a grave injustice, however. Aligoté wines can be every bit as varied as those of other grape varieties depending on where the grapes are grown within the Bourgogne-Aligoté appellation. Haute-Côtes wines are lively; those from St-Bris, in the *département* of the Yonne, reveal a touch of elderflower reminiscent of Sauvignon Blanc.

Cabernet franc

Where Bordeaux wines are concerned, Cabernet Sauvignon and Merlot have a tendency to steal all the limelight. However, both history and literature agree that the delightful Cabernet Franc deserves a prize for best supporting role.

Vineyard profile

Cabernet Franc is a low-yield grape variety that in the Bordeaux region barely produces 40 hectolitres per hectare. In the Languedoc methods of long-pruning have proved more productive, boosting output to as much as 80 hectolitres per hectare. The Languedoc wines are deep in colour with an alcohol content of 11 per cent abv. Bud burst occurs around 10 days earlier than in the companion variety, Cabernet Sauvignon. Cabernet Franc vines are susceptible to downy mildew, powdery mildew and grey rot and their leaves may become pockmarked with phylloxera galls. More vigorous than Cabernet Sauvignon, Cabernet Franc vines have an average yield of 40 hectolitres per hectare and require long-pruning to encourage productivity.

In France

Cabernet Franc covers 45,000 hectares of vineyards worldwide. Of these, nearly 36,000 hectares are in mainland France, where it is cultivated in two main regions: the southwest (especially in the *départements* of the Gironde and the Dordogne) and the west (Anjou and Touraine). In the southwest, Cabernet Franc is blended with Cabernet Sauvignon and Merlot; in Anjou and Touraine it is planted alongside Gamay, Côt and Cabernet Sauvignon. Cabernet Franc vines were recently introduced to Mediterranean vineyards, where they now cover several hundred hectares. In Bordeaux, Cabernet Franc complements blends of Cabernet Sauvignon and Merlot and is mainly planted on the right bank of the Dordogne and Gironde rivers. It

excels in the area around Libourne, where the warm sand and gravel soils provide ideal conditions for maturation and ensure the delicate structure of the finished wines. Château Cheval Blanc, on the boundary of the gravel soils of Pomerol, is notable for growing an unusually high proportion of Cabernet Franc. Wines produced here can be cellared for long periods, while also being sufficiently rich in elegant, rounded tannins to be suitable for early drinking. In the southwest, the AOVDQS red and rosé Coteaux du Quercy wines give full expression to Cabernet Franc's character. It is the dominant grape variety in the area, more prevalent than Tannat, Cot, Gamay and Merlot. The resulting wines are deep crimson in colour, fleshy and flavourful. Other AOC denominations are Pécharmant,

Thanks to Cabernet Franc, Bourgueil wines have been highly respected since the 16th century. Today, the Bourgueil appellation includes the vineyards of Château d'Ingrandes, shown here.

Côtes-de-Duras and Buzet. However Anjou and Touraine supply the most authentic expression of Cabernet Franc, in the wines of Saumur-Champigny, St-Nicolas-de-Bourgueil, Bourgueil and Chinon.

This ancient grape variety left the land of Aquitaine for the Loire Valley where it became known as the *Plant Breton*. The reason why remains a mystery to ampelographers. Back in the 16th century, Rabelais remarked in his *Ecris*: 'of this good Breton wine not a sign in Brittany, only in the fine lands of Véron' (situated between the river Loire and Vienne). At the start of the 17th century, Cardinal de Richelieu, who had inherited the Abbaye de St-Nicolas-de-Bourgueil, also commented on the admirable quality of this vine from Guyenne, immediately instructing his steward, the Abbé Breton, to commence plantings on the Cardinal's estates of Chinon and Bourgueil. This explains why notarial acts of the time began to specify whether the young plants growing in walled vineyards had been planted by the Abbé Breton or were simply *Plant Breton* vines.

Around the world

In Italy, plantings of Cabernet Franc date from the 19th century when the country was under Hapsburg rule. The first vines were planted in the Friuli region of northeast Italy, although there is some confusion as to what proportion of these were actually Cabernet Franc's blending companion Cabernet Sauvignon. However, Cabernet Franc vines today account for the larger share, with an estimated 6,000 hectares planted throughout Italy. Wines produced here are low in tannins, popular with consumers and ready for drinking after two or three years' cellaring. Cabernet Franc also does well in eastern Europe, particularly in former Yugoslavia and Hungary. It also has proved successful in Australia where it covers 7,500 hectares of vineyards, and is cultivated to a lesser extent in South Africa, New Zealand and Argentina. In the United States, where Cabernet Franc was for many years confused with Merlot, vineyardists now achieve excellent results with Cabernet Franc in the states of California (860 hectares), Washington and New York.

Colour and Taste

Cabernet Franc wines are less deeply coloured than the Cabernet Sauvignons and, being less tannic, are quicker to mature. Grapes grown on chalky *tuffeau* (limestone) or argillaceous-sandstone terrain produce wines with an intensely aromatic bouquet of raspberries, violets and liquorice. Cabernet Franc cultivated in colder climates tends to produce wines that are paler in colour and somewhat vegetal in quality, with distinct aromas of sweet peppers.

Between the Loire and Vienne: The pride of Touraine

The name of Cabernet Franc is celebrated in the wines of Bourgueil, Saint-Nicolas-de-Bourgueil and Chinon. The Bourgueil region distinguishes between *vins de tuf* (wines made from grapes planted in *tuffeau*) and *vins de terrasses* (wines produced from grapes planted on terraces). The former are well structured and slightly austere in youth but can mature in the cellar for five years or more. The latter are highly aromatic, developing notes of cherries and strawberries that make them more attractive in youth than the *vins de tuf*. Chinon wines are a delicate ruby-red, with a supple palate and an elegant nose allying scents of red berries with soft fruits.

Also known as …

Being such a widespread wine, Cabernet Franc has many synonyms. In Bordeaux dialect, Cabernet Sauvignon and Cabernet Franc are both known as Petite Vidure and Bidure. In Chinon and the Vienne it is known as Breton, Plant Breton or Plant de l'Abbé. In the Bordeaux region, some *vignerons* in St-Emilion call it Bouchet or Gros Bouchet; those in the Médoc call it Gros Cabernet or Grosse Vidure, and *vignerons* in Madiran call it Bouchy.

Identifying the grape variety

Cabernet Franc has a felty white growing tip with a crimson border. The leaves are orbicular and smooth, glossy light green in colour with five well-defined lobes and small, narrow teeth. The petiolar sinus is lyre-shaped and the underside of the blade is cobwebby. The bunches of grapes are small, almost conical in shape, sometimes with a small wing, and packed with spherical, blue-black grapes that taste sweet and slightly astringent at the same time.

Opposite: the wines of Château Cheval-Blanc in St-Emilion owe their unique characteristics to the predominance of Cabernet Franc planted on ancient gravels.

Right: La Devinière in the Chinon region, birthplace of the famous Renaissance humanist François Rabelais, circa 1495. Rabelais was among the first to sing the praises of Cabernet Franc.

Cabernet sauvignon

Cabernet Sauvignon is the Médoc grape variety *par excellence*, imparting character to all the Grands Crus produced on the left bank of the Gironde. It is also established in Spain and widely cultivated throughout the New World. Originally from Bordeaux, Cabernet Sauvignon is one of the finest representatives of French noble grape varieties and is cultivated with success in vineyards around the world.

Vineyard profile

It is widely recognised that one of Cabernet Sauvignon's most distinguishable characteristics is its taste of peppers, which is more or less marked according to the *terroir* on which it is grown. Few people know, however, that the origins of this taste lie in an ancient hybrid of Sauvignon Blanc and Cabernet Franc. Cabernet Sauvignon has an upright growing habit with flexible shoots that suit various training methods. It is also a highly adaptable grape variety. Thanks to late bud burst there is little danger from treacherous springtime frosts. Additionally, towards the end of the season as the harvest approaches, the grapes are quite large enough to withstand rot, should the weather turn wet. But despite its dependable performance in different *terroirs*, Cabernet Sauvignon can only produce premium wines if yields are kept in check. For this reason,

conscientious *vignerons* frequently carry out green harvests in the summer, thinning the grape bunches to reduce the crop. In the Bordeaux region the finest wines come from old vines whose grapes yield beautifully concentrated juice. Young, vigorous vines on the other hand can produce more than 70 hectolitres per hectare, but the wine is second rate and can never be used in the Grands Crus. Vineyardists in the New World (e.g. in the Napa Valley in California) and in Catalonia in Spain, also limit yields to ensure the quality of their wines. Naturally, less severe pruning will produce a bigger crop and in hot climates producers irrigate their vines to boost yields still further. The quality of the wines obtained, though, is mediocre.

In France

In 1999 Cabernet Sauvignon covered 51,442 hectares of French vineyards, ranking fifth in the

classification of French grape varieties. It is planted in four main regions: Aquitaine, the southwest, the south and the Loire. Plantings of Cabernet Sauvignon in Aquitaine cover 33,160 hectares and represent 52 per cent of vineyard production. While not as widely planted as it was in the past, Cabernet Sauvignon remains the embodiment of the great Médoc wines. It does best on the warm gravel soils that slope gently down to the Gironde, offering good drainage and preventing rain water from collecting around the roots. In the Haut Médoc, which extends from Blanquefort to St-Seurin-de-Cadourne, six communal appellations produce the most celebrated wines of the Bordeaux region: Listrac-Médoc, Moulis-en-Médoc, Margaux, Pauillac, St-Estèphe and St-Julien. The Médoc was at the forefront of viticulture in the 18th century as local vineyard owners rapidly became aware of the critical relationship between *terroir* and the quality of wine. This prompted the syndicate of brokers to establish the 1855 Classification of Bordeaux, which preceded other regional classifications by nearly a century. Cabernet Sauvignon was the first grape to benefit from these developments.

In the southwest, particularly around Bergerac and Buzet, Cabernet Sauvignon is planted as a secondary grape variety for red (and sometimes rosé) blended wines. In the south of France it is mainly used

in the shadow of the Andes, this Chilean vine grows in a succession of valleys of varying sandy soils. This red grape is the most widely grown variety after Pais and Semillon.

in the production of *vins de pays*, covering 11,844 hectares of vineyards in the Languedoc and 4,349 hectares in Provence. Here, some of the plantings are in AOC areas such as the Côtes-de-Provence and the Coteaux-d'Aix-en-Provence. In the Loire Valley (2,067 hectares) Cabernet Sauvignon is a secondary grape variety that is used to vinify red and rosé wines produced by the appellations of Anjou, Bourgueil, Chinon, Saumur and Touraine. Cabernet Sauvignon also complements Cabernet Franc in Cabernet-d'Anjou and Cabernet-de-Saumur rosé wines.

Around the world

Thanks to the excellent quality of its wines, Cabernet Sauvignon is the most widespread red wine grape after Merlot. It covers 165,000 hectares of vineyards worldwide in Spain, Italy, the former Yugoslavia, Romania, Bulgaria, Moldavia, South Africa, the United States, Chile and Australia. Cabernet Sauvignon success stories are legion. In Spain it is the source of the great Gran Coronas Etiqueta Negra created by Catalan producer Miguel Torres, who devotes 29 hectares of his renowned Mas La Plana vineyard in Penedès to Cabernet Sauvignon. The vines, with an average age of about 20 years, are planted on fluvial terraces and gravels where they produce concentrated grapes that are picked at night to preserve the unique aromas. The wine is matured first in new American and French oak casks, followed by a further 12 months ageing in second or third generation barrels, thus in the process acquiring magnificent structure and velvety smoothness.

In California, Cabernet Sauvignon was the focus of a fine example of cooperation in viniculture. In 1979 the wine producer Robert Mondavi formed a partnership with Baron Philippe de Rothschild, the French owner of Château Mouton-Rothschild in Pauillac. That same year also saw the announcement of their first vintage vinified by Timothy Mondavi and Lucien Sionneau, cellar master at Château Mouton-Rothschild. Four years later on from this, the two celebrated wine producers founded Opus One, planted with typically Médoc grape varieties, in Oakville, Napa Valley. Before long, the new estate was producing one of the most prestigious wines in the United States. Cabernet Sauvignon accounts for 80–97 per cent of the blend, complemented, depending on the year, by Cabernet Franc, Merlot or occasionally Malbec. Matured in French oak casks for slightly less than 20 months, Opus One is a robust wine, as complex on the nose as it is on the palate, with distinct aromas of spice remaining from the wood, coupled with delicate notes of violet and lingering hints of mint. With age, it grows more supple and becomes more distinguished.

Colour and Taste

Provided yields are restricted, Cabernet Sauvignon produces deeply coloured wines of characteristically tannic nature, even in their youth. In the classified growths of the Médoc, these tannins are further enhanced by periods of ageing in new oak (usually from the celebrated forest of Tronçay in the *département* of Allier). After a few years, depending on the vintage and the cru, the wine develops a network of delicate tannins opening on complex aromas of ripe blackcurrant, cedar and spices. The aroma of peppers, meanwhile, though typical of Cabernet Sauvignon, is not necessarily a sign of quality and, if too intense, suggests under-ripe grapes and can leave a disagreeable vegetal taste. In the Médoc, Cabernet Sauvignon grapes are never vinified on their own but usually represent three-quarters of the final blend, the balance being made up by Cabernet Franc, Merlot or Petit Verdot.

Opposite: Château Lafite-Rothschild in Pauillac, where Cabernet Sauvignon represents 70 per cent of plantings and expresses its full elegance in the celebrated wines that are produced there.

Pauillac: strength and elegance

Cabernet Sauvignon is the dominant grape variety in the Pauillac appellation, home of magnificent deep red wines that can be laid down and enjoyed many years later on. The typical bouquet echoes notes of blackcurrant coupled with aromas of leather and a hint of vanilla, liquorice and roasting coffee beans from the oak. While slightly austere in youth, Pauillac wine softens with time into an undeniably fine and complex mouthful.

Identifying the grape variety

Cabernet Sauvignon has a downy white growing tip with a crimson border. The leaves are orbicular and glossy dark green in colour, and they become slightly red in autumn. The blade has a bullate surface, five sharply defined lobes and a closed, lyre-shaped petiolar sinus. The underside of the blade feels downy to the touch. The grape bunches are small-to-medium size, conical and sometimes with a small wing. The grapes are small, black and spherical with a thick coating of bloom that gives them a bluish hue. A tough outer skin covers crisp flesh with a characteristic flavour of wild fruits such as sorb-apples.

Also known as...

Cabernet Sauvignon is known colloquially by a variety of names. In Bordeaux dialect they call it Vidure (from *bois dur* meaning 'hard wood'), Petite Vidure and Vidure Sauvignonne. In the Dordogne it is called Navarre; in St-Emilion, Bouchet; in the Libourne region, Bouschet-Sauvignon; in Castillon-la-Bataille, Marchoupet; in the Bazadais region, Carbouet. *Vignerons* in the Graves sometimes refer to it as Sauvignonne, and in the Médoc it is just Sauvignon. In central France, surprised visitors may well be offered a glass of Sauvignon Rouge. In Russia and Bulgaria, Kaberne-Sovinjon is known as Lafite or Lafet, no doubt because of its association with the celebrated Château Lafite. Similarly, the Spanish also refer to it as Burdeos Tinto (red Bordeaux).

Carignan

Few grape varieties have been more sadly neglected than Carignan. This much maligned grape has been largely confined to low-lying, mass-production vineyards that stifle its natural potential. And yet with age and planted in good *terroirs*, Carignan can yield wines bursting with character.

Vineyard profile

Carignan is a vigorous grower with very tough shoots. Due to late bud burst, it easily escapes early frosts but as a late-maturing vine it needs a Mediterranean climate to thrive. Production varies greatly according to region of growth and method of training: from 30–70 hectolitres per hectare on the slopes, to 200 hectolitres per hectare on flat land. Carignan is also notoriously susceptible to powdery mildew, which encourages rot to develop on the grape bunches.

In France

Carignan is a red grape variety that originated in Aragon in Spain, where it was cultivated around the town of Cariñena (the grape's Spanish synonym). Introduced in France in the 12th century, it soon became the most widely cultivated grape variety in the country. Despite massive uprooting in recent years which has reduced plantings by half, it still covers more than 102,000 hectares of French vineyards. The three main areas are Languedoc-Roussillon, Provence and Corsica. Until the end of the 1970s, it became increasingly popular throughout the Languedoc as a source of

mass-produced wines. Like Aramon which it gradually supplanted, Carignan seemed destined for blending with strong Algerian wines to supply the needs of the large industrial towns in the north via the railways. The wines produced were fairly high in alcohol, often acidic and quite unremarkable.

Today *vignerons* in the Languedoc respect the distinctive characteristics of Carignan by planting old vine plants on slopes and in well-exposed argillaceous-limestone soils, sandy gravels and schist. Carignan grapes consequently remain the dominant variety in the Côtes-de-Provence, Costières-de-Nîmes, Faugères, Minervois, Fitou, St-Chinian, Corbières and the Côtes-du-Roussillon. They are usually blended with Grenache Noir, Cinsaut, Syrah and sometimes

Mourvèdre. Carignan accounts for 60-70 per cent of wines produced in Fitou, where the vines do well on the schists of the Villeneuve and Cascatel basins, and in the red argillaceous-limestone of coastal regions.

Left: Château de Jau in Roussillon – Carignan blended with Syrah and Grenache Noir produces Côtes-du-Roussillon wines. Below: the village of Minerve, after which the Minervois appellation is named.

Around the world

Contrary to expectation, Carignan (or Mazuelo, as it is also known in Spain) is no longer widely cultivated in Spain: these wines today contain more Grenache than Carignan. That said, it still covers 8,100 hectares of vineyard and is a recommended grape variety in the Basque country, Navarra, Rioja and Aragon and most especially, in Catalonia. The small Catalan wine zone of Priorato nestles in a protective corrie of hills. The climate is temperate and fairly dry; the meagre soils are a mixture of slate and quartz known locally as *licorella*. Carignan remains the dominant grape variety, but Grenache is becoming more widespread. Wines are deeply coloured with developing aromas of ripe fruits. In Italy, Carignan has been awarded its own *denominazione d'origine controllata* (DOC): Carignano del Sulcis, a red or rosé, still or sparkling wine from the Sardinian province of Cagliari. Carignan is also cultivated in other parts of the world and currently covers more than 160,000 hectares in Tunisia, Morocco, California, Mexico, Argentina, Uruguay, Australia (in the Barossa Valley), China and even India (in south Bengal).

The small isolated wine region of Priorato in Catalonia produces great red wines from Carignan and Grenache.

Côtes-du-Roussillon

Carignan is 60 per cent of the blend in Côtes-du-Roussillon wines. Their bouquet has an unmistakable spiciness, coupled with flavours of morellos and blackcurrants from the Grenache element, and violets from the Syrah. Carignan thrives in the varied soils of Côtes-du-Roussillon: argillaceous-limestone soils in Tautavel, pebbly terraces in Albères and schists in the Maury Valley. Tautavel and Albères wines are generous and strong, and made for laying down. The schistous soils on the other hand produce supple wines suitable for early drinking.

Colour and Taste

Carignan produces robust, deeply coloured wines that are high in alcohol (more than 12 per cent) and acidity. For best results, the wines are vinified using carbonic maceration: uncrushed grapes are placed in vats containing carbon dioxide which causes them to ferment inside the unbroken skins and so releases their aromatic constituents. The resulting wines are similar in bouquet and texture to Corbières de Boutenac wines that are blended from Carignan and Grenache. Côtes-du-Roussillon wines have an aroma of red berries mixed with spicy notes and the fragrance of the *garrigue* (the wild-herb-covered land of the region). Their texture is supported by supple tannins with no trace of bitterness.

Identifying the grape variety

Carignan has a felty white growing tip and large, orbicular, very crimped leaves with five serrated lobes. The underside of the blade has a cobwebby appearance. The grape bunches are winged, quite large, cylindrical-conical. The blue-black grapes produced have a thick, quite bitter-tasting skin, and sweet but rather flavourless juice.

Also known as...

Carignan is known as Carignane, Carigane Noire, Carignano, Carinena and Calignan. It is also called Bois Dur (hard wood), Bois de Fer (iron wood), Plant d'Espagne (Spanish vine) and Roussillonen. *Vignerons* in the Aude refer to it as Catalan and in the Gard they call it Mataro. To Spanish vineyardists it is Cariñena, Crujillón or Mazuelo. To the Italians it is Carignano or Legno Duro (especially in Tuscany).

The imposing, legendary Cathare citadel of Queribus, which dominates the Côtes-du-Roussillon landscape.

Chardonnay

There is scarcely a wine region on earth that does not include plantings of Chardonnay, the great Burgundian grape variety to which we owe that most famous of all white wines, Montrachet. Far and wide, this celebrated grape has been adapted to various *terroirs* by *vignerons* who have come to associate it with fine, powerfully aromatic wines.

Vineyard profile

Chardonnay is particularly vulnerable to spring frosts, so vineyard conditions must be carefully managed to control the risk. The vines are long-pruned according to the Guyot system and *vignerons* in Burgundy, like those in Champagne, use *chaufferettes* (little heaters) and *aspersion* (spraying the young shoots with water to form a protective coat of ice against extremely cold air) to protect the emerging buds from late March to early April. Heavy rainfall or a drop in temperature in May brings the risk of *coulure* (non-setting of fruit).

The unmistakable hill of Corton, above Aloxe-Corton in the Côte de Beaune, with its dark cap of woods. Corton Grand Cru vines are grown on top slopes, with the Premier Cru vines lower down.

In France

Chardonnay is largely absent from southwest and central France but elsewhere plantings have increased considerably in the past 10 years rising from 19,870 hectares in 1988 to 35,123 hectares in 1999. Chardonnay is the No 1 white grape variety in Burgundy, where it originated (its red counterpart is Pinot Noir). It is the source of the great dry white wines of the Côte d'Or, including such masterpieces as Montrachet, Meursault and Corton-Charlemagne, which send prices rocketing at wine auctions. Chablis, too, owes as much to Chardonnay grapes as it does to the celebrated argillaceous-limestone marls of the Kimmeridgian, containing numerous fossils of the comma-shaped oyster, *Exogyra virgula*. To the west of Mâcon, Chardonnay reveals another side to its character

on the soils of Pouilly-Fuissé and the twinned *terroirs* of Pouilly-Loché and Pouilly-Vinzelles. These communes are famous for dry, pleasing wines produced from vines planted at the foot of the limestone escarpments of Solutré and Vergisson. In the Stone Age, these prow-shaped rocks were home to a remarkable tribe of stone carvers and horse hunters.

Further north, Chardonnay accounts for 27 per cent of land under vine in Champagne, principally on the Côte des Blancs, the chalky, relatively sheltered slopes to the south of Epernay, where Blanc de Blancs Champagnes (made exclusively from Chardonnay and not from a blend of red – Pinot Noir and Pinot Meunier – and white grapes) predominate. However Chardonnay is by no means a northern grape variety, as we see in the Langedoc, where it is blended with varying proportions of Mauzac and Chenin to produce the distinctive sparkling and still white Limoux wines, including the famous Crémant-de-Limoux. Elsewhere we find Chardonnay used to make Crémant-d'Alsace in Alsace, white wine in the Jura (blended with Savagnin) and white wine in Anjou

(blended with 20 per cent Sauvignon Blanc).

Around the world

There is probably not a wine region in the world without Chardonnay. Plantings worldwide currently exceed 130,000 hectares and could well reach 150,000 hectares by the next decade. The wines produced are as varied as the countries that produce them. Italy used to confuse Chardonnay with Pinot Blanc but no longer; with around 11,800 hectares of Chardonnay, the country has acquired a fine reputation for its cask-matured Trentino and Friuli wines. Chardonnay is also used to make *spumante*. In Piedmont, producer Angelo Gaja's respected Gaia vineyard, at an altitude of more than 400 m (1,300 ft), is entirely planted with Chardonnay. Vinified on lees, the wines undergo a second fermentation, called malolactic fermentation, in new oak casks. The result is a wine with a concentrated bouquet of vanilla, fresh butter and praline coupled with a fruity palate of elegant acidity. In Spain, the sparkling wine *cava*, which is made principally in Catalonia by the traditional method, may also contain a proportion of Chardonnay. Burgenland in Austria is famous for the quality of its viscous Chardonnay wines and Romania for its late-harvested Chardonnays from Murfatlar region. Plantings of Chardonnay have soared on the other side of the

Atlantic. There is now more Chardonnay grown in the United States (over 36,000 hectares) than in the whole of France. Most of this is in California, in the cooler regions of the Napa Valley, Sonoma and Monterey, where conditions are favourable for the grape. Washington State, traditionally famous for its Riesling and Sémillon wines, also turned to Chardonnay at the end of the 1980s. Chardonnay is also cultivated in Argentina, Chile (in the Casablanca Valley), New Zealand and especially Australia, where plantings continue to rise steadily. Throughout the world, the Burgundian grape has become the symbol of quality in viticulture, and the key to conquering new markets abroad.

Colour and Taste

Still or sparkling, dry or sweet, Chardonnay wines have a distinctive elegance which is supported by well-judged acidity and an intense

range of aromas. Both in the New World countries that took their inspiration from the great Burgundian dry white wines and in Burgundy itself, Chardonnay is softened by the process of malolactic fermentation followed by ageing in oak barrels. The complexity of the bouquet varies according to the *terroir*. Chablis wines have aromas of gun flint, lime blossom and white-fleshed fruits (peaches, pears, lychees), while those of the Côte d'Or offer scents of butter and acacia honey. Between the two extremes, a gamut of aromatic nuances distinguishes one cru from another. The Blanc de Blancs are the finest and freshest of all Champagnes, with characteristic Chardonnay flavours of toast, butter, brioche, hazelnuts and straw against a background of white-fleshed fruits and lemony citrus. Chardonnay wines are also distinguished by their magnificent luminous green highlights.

Corton-Charlemagne

This legendary Burgundian dry white wine from the top of the Montagne de Corton is pale gold with green reflections in youth. The bouquet reveals rich aromas of baked apples lightly brushed with butter, lime blossom, honey, cinnamon and citrus. The generous, well-structured palate is the mark of a wine that may be laid down for 20 years.

Opposite above:

Chablis vineyards in the north of Burgundy, home to a wine that is universally renowned for its fruity fragrance, date back to the 12th century and the foundation of the Cistercian abbey of Pontigny.

Below: Chardonnay vines flourish south of San Francisco in the county of Monterey, USA, in a paradoxical climate so dry that it depends on irrigation but is cooled by refreshing breezes.

Identifying the grape variety
Chardonnay is frequently referred to as the white version of Pinot Noir, with which it is cultivated in Burgundy, but it is distinguishable from the latter by the shape of its leaves. The Chardonnay growing tip is downy white with a crimson border. The leaves are orbicular and a bright, light green colour with a delicately bullate surface. The blade is trilobate but poorly defined with revolute edges and a lyre-shaped, naked, petiolar sinus. The grape bunches are cylindrical in shape, sometimes with two wings; the grapes may be spherical or slightly oblong, turning amber-yellow in the sun, thin-skinned, with soft, sweet, fairly substantial flesh.

Also known as...
Chardonnay is known by a variety of names that explain why it has been confused with grape varieties such as Pinot Blanc, Chenin and Melon. It is known as Morillon Blanc around Paris; Chardonnet, Chardenay or Chaudenet on the Côte Chalonnaise in Burgundy; Rousseau or Roussot in the Yonne; Noirien Blanc on the Côte d'Or; and Beaunois near Tonnerre. *Vignerons* in Champagne know Chardonnay as Epinette in the Marne and Arboisier in the Aube, while to those in the Jura it is called Melon Blanc and Melon d'Arbois.

Chasselas

There's a commune in the Mâconnais called Chasselas, which claims that the Chasselas grape originated there. However, as man started to travel the world, alternative stories about the origins of this modest white variety of grape began to emerge.

The royal vine

One tale suggests that Chasselas had been cultivated since time immemorial around Constantinople. Then in 1536, in the rule of François I, after the signature of the treaty of commerce with Turkey, an ambassador is said to have returned to France with Chasselas canes. These were planted in the château of Fontainebleu and in Thomery, producing grapes for a wine that was popular with the royal court. Later, in the reign of Louis XV, a certain General Courten returned to Switzerland with young Chasselas vines originating from Fontainebleu. Impossible, say the historians, since the celebrated royal vine was only planted around 1750. The Swiss hypothesis holds that in the Middle Ages, Cistercian monks cultivated Fendant grapes (the Swiss name for Chasselas) on the slopes of Dézaley from where it spread throughout the cantons of Vaud to Geneva, Neuchâtel, Lake Biel and the Valais. According to this story, the royal vine has its origins in Chasselas vines brought back between 1515 and 1830 by Swiss soldiers in the French army, many of whom were *vignerons*.

Vineyard profile

Chasselas bud burst occurs early, exposing the developing plant to the risk of spring frosts. The vines are goblet-pruned without training on wires in the south of France, but supported by a central stake in Switzerland. Some vineyards also use Cordon de Royat or Cordon de Guyot pruning, training the shoots on horizontal wires. Chasselas grapes are suitable for both table grapes and wine grapes but yields vary greatly depending on methods of cultivation and types of soil. The finest table grapes are grown on the thin soils of the slopes of Tarn-et-Garonne in the Chasselas de Moissac AOC.

In France

Pouilly-sur-Loire, Alsace, Crépy and Savoie are the French regions most representative of Chasselas. Table grapes account for some 3,500 hectares of the area under vine, wine grapes slightly less than 500 hectares. In Pouilly-sur-Loire, *vignerons* increasingly prefer Sauvignon Blanc to Chasselas, which they find too unreliable and vulnerable to weather conditions. In Alsace, Chasselas is blended with Pinot Blanc, Auxerrois and especially Sylvaner to produce Edelzwicker wine. *Vignerons* near Colmar used to produce sweet, straw-coloured wines (*Strohwein*) called the *Vins des Trois Rois* (the Three Kings) using over-ripened grapes dried on straw-covered frames. Today Chasselas does best of all in Savoie on the banks of Lake Geneva, source of the light and often slightly sparkling Marin, Ripaille and Marignan wines.

In Switzerland

Chasselas, known locally as Fendant, is Switzerland's leading grape variety covering nearly 5,600 hectares, or 30 per cent of Swiss vineyards. It extends throughout the canton of Vaud, in prime position on the terraces overlooking Lake Geneva, La Côte, Lavaux, Chablais and other communes. The landscape here is entirely composed of vineyards planted on steep slopes that catch the sun. In the Valais, the Chasselas grapes grown on the steep banks of the Rhône impose their characteristic mark on the crus of Sion, Martigny and Chamoson. Chasselas is also the dominant grape variety in the cantons of Geneva, Neuchâtel and Berne, on the left bank of Lake Biel at the foot of the Jura.

Around the world

In Germany, Chasselas was first planted at the start of the 17th century in Württemberg and Franconia, then in Sachsen and Baden a century later. Chasselas vines are widespread throughout eastern Europe, also in the Iberian peninsula, Italy, Algeria, Lebanon and Israel. In the New World, Chasselas is grown in Chile, California and New Zealand.

Colour and Taste

The typical Chasselas wine is slightly sparkling and crisp, finishing with a pleasantly sharp sensation. The aromas are equally distinctive, blending notes of lime blossom with elegant floral touches and even occasional mineral nuances reflecting the *terroir*.

Dézaley

At the heart of the spectacular Lavaux region in Switzerland, the vineyards of Dézaley benefit from the *deux soleils* (two suns): direct sunlight combines with sun reflected off Lake Geneva to heat up the small terrace walls. Dézaley wine is pale yellow with fragrant notes of honey and flowers and has a well-balanced richness, thanks to the characteristic liveliness of Chasselas.

Identifying the grape variety

Chasselas has a cobwebby, white growing tip. The leaves are red at first, developing into smooth, light green with five deeply defined lobes. Grape bunches are cylindrical with spherical, light green to amber-yellow grapes that turn reddish-brown in the sun. The skin is thin but tough, and the flesh, juicy and succulent.

Also known as...

Being so widespread the Chasselas grape has become associated with several place names. Mostly it is known as Mornen in the Rhône and the Aine regions; Fendant, Fendant Roux or Fendant Vert in Switzerland; and Weisser Gutedel in Germany.

Opposite: The Moissac vineyard, granted AOC status for the production of Chasselas table grapes. Right: the Dézaley vineyards on the banks of Lake Geneva in the canton of Vaud, where the vines are planted on steep terraces.

Chenin

Despite the link suggested with the Clos du Mont Chenin in Cormery, Touraine, Chenin was first planted in Anjou in the 9th century and did not appear in vineyards around Tour until the start of the 15th century. Also called Pineau de la Loire, Chenin is a white grape variety thought to be descended from the red grape Pineau d'Aunis, which was also known as Chenin Noir.

Vineyard profile

Bud burst occurs early in Chenin, exposing it to the risk of spring frosts. As the Chenin vine is a heterogeneous variety, *vignerons* in Anjou choose early-ripening clones, which they plant in favourably exposed positions on pebbly soils that warm up quickly. Chenin grapes are susceptible to noble rot (*Botrytis cinerea*) and thus particularly suitable for producing the great sweet wines. These days *vignerons* allow the grapes to dry out on the vines (a process known as *passerillage* or raisining) or pick the grapes in successive batches once they have become botrytised.

In France

Apart from limited quantities in the Languedoc, where it is grown alongside Mauzac and Chardonnay to produce Blanquette-de-Limoux, Chenin performs best in the Loire Valley, which accounts for the majority of plantings in France (9,500 hectares). The wines produced here vary greatly depending on whether they come from Anjou or Touraine, ranging from dry, white, lively and even sparkling, to sweet (*liquoreux*). In Anjou, Chenin grapes have a reputation for sweet (*moelleux*) wines such as Coteaux-du-Layon, Bonnezeaux and Quarts-de-Chaume, each reflecting the character of the grape variety, as well as the *terroir*. However, Chenin has also gained respectability as the source of some excellent dry white

Golden, overripe
Chenin grapes.

wines. The crus of Savennières, Coulée-de-Serrant and Roche-aux-Moines are planted at the foot of schistous slopes, where the mild microclimate is tempered by the closeness of the river Loire, producing wines of enormous complexity. In the Anjou appellation, Chenin today is also the basis of dry wines blended with 20 per cent Chardonnay and Sauvignon Blanc. Other appellations growing Chenin are Saumur, Vouvray, Montlouis and even the Coteaux-du-Loir and Jasnières. Wines that leave the cool *tuffeau* (calcareous rock) cellars deep in the Loire Valley may be dry,

medium-dry, sweet, still and, since the end of the 19th century, sparkling or slightly sparkling. This depends on the year and each vineyard's proximity to the river Loire.

Around the world

Chenin is particularly popular in South Africa, where it may have been planted by the first commander of Cape Town in 1655, three years after he set up a trading post there.

Known as Steen, Chenin grapes account for nearly 30 per cent (28,000 hectares) of the vineyards in South Africa, where the

Mediterranean-style climate is quite unlike the mild climate in Anjou, and leads to mass-produced, quaffable wines with a tendency to flabbiness. The same is true in California (which grows the same amount of Chenin as France) and Argentina, and even in Australia and New Zealand. Total plantings of Chenin worldwide are over 53,000 hectares.

Colour and Taste

The sweet wines based on Chenin offer aromas of honey, acacia, quince and crystallised fruits, characteristic of overripe grapes. These full-bodied, often quite strong wines vary in colour from yellow with green reflections for Anjou-Coteaux-de-la-Loire, to deep gold for Coteaux-du-Layon. Deeper tones are associated with botrytised grapes that owe their high sugar content to the fungus *Botrytis cinerea* rather than to *passerillage sur souche* (raisining on the vine). With age, the wines take on more amber nuances. Thanks to high acidity, Chenin wine ages well, with some of the best sweet wines still drinkable after 40 years or more in the great vintages. Dry Chenin wines combine roundness and liveliness with citrus aromas. Those from Savennières are distinguished by a subtle bouquet: aromas of white flowers such as acacia and lime blossom together with mineral notes, finishing with a slight bitterness characteristic of the *terroir*.

White grapes account for around two-thirds of production in South Africa, where plantings of Chenin even exceed those of Colombard.

Bonnezeaux

The rich, sweet wines of Bonnezeaux are produced from Chenin vines planted on steep south-facing, schistous slopes above the village of Thouarcé on the right-bank of the river Layon. Harvesting occurs at the end of October when the grapes have had time to shrivel on the vine, thus concentrating their sugars. This yields an intensely sweet, golden yellow wine. The bouquet is refined, with aromas of dried exotic and citrus fruits, ripe pears and white flowers.

Identifying the grape variety

Chenin has a felty white growing tip with a crimson border. The leaves are dark green, orbicular and bullate with five sharply defined lobes. Chenins petiolar sinus is lyre-shaped and the underside of the blade is downy. The grape bunches are conical in shape, with one or two wings and the grapes are densely packed together, favouring the development of noble rot. A delicate golden-yellow skin covers dense flesh.

Also known as...

The most common synonyms for Chenin are Pineau – or Pinot – in the Loire in France, and Steen in South Africa. *Vignerons* in the Gard sometimes also refer to Chenin as Ugne Lombarde.

Vineyards around the village of Thouarcé in the Bonnezeaux appellation are situated on the pebbly schistous slopes of La Montagne, Beauregard and Fesles.

Cinsaut

Cinsaut, the Mediterranean grape variety *par excellence*, can give supple, fruity wines. However like Carignan, it suffered from the excesses of mass-production and, for a time, lost the confidence of winegrowers.

The Coteaux-Varois

Cinsaut is the dominant grape variety in these radiant pink rosé wines from Provence, which have the colour of rose petals, aromas of berries and soft fruits (peaches, raspberries and strawberries) and a lively, yet soft palate.

The vineyards of Coteaux-Varois.

Vineyard profile

Cinsaut is a moderately vigorous variety characterised by a spreading habit, late bud burst and a vulnerability to numerous pests and diseases. While the grapes are suitable for both wine and table grapes, Cinsaut table grapes (known as *Œillade*) are mainly confined to French markets because they are considered too small to be exported commercially.

In France

French plantings of Cinsaut have

Identifying the grape variety

Cinsaut has a felty white growing tip with a crimson border. The leaves are light green, orbicular, with five deeply defined lobes. The grape bunches are large, cylindrical-conical and compact. The grapes are large, blue-black in colour, with juicy but quite firm flesh.

fallen significantly since the 1980s – just 32,000 hectares at the dawn of the new millennium compared with 51,648 in 1979. For many years Cinsaut cultivation centred on low-lying vineyards in the Languedoc where excessively high yields brought this variety into disrepute. This prompted *vignerons* to replace Cinsaut with more noble grape varieties such as Syrah and Mourvèdre. Nevertheless, Cinsaut blended with Carignan and Grenache gives convincing results in the red wines of Minervois and even Corbières, where it is planted on poor, dry soils and where yields are limited to 45 hectolitres per hectare. Cinsaut is also one of the 13 grape varieties permitted in the Châteauneuf-du-Pape AOC. Additionally, it contributes to many rosé wines including Coteux-du-Languedoc-Cabrières, Côtes-du-Rhône, Lirac and Tavel wines and Provençal appellations including the Coteaux-Varois.

Also known as...

Cinsaut is known as Hermitage in South Africa and Black Malvoisie in California. In France it is called Cinsault, Cinqsaut or Cinq-Saou in the Languedoc; Plant d'Arles in the Bouches-du-Rhône; Bourdalès in the Pyrénées Orientales; Picardan Noir in the Var; Espagnen in the Vaucluse; and Salerne in Nice. The table grapes of Cinsaut are known as Œillades.

Around the world

Algerian plantings of Cinsaut have also fallen considerably but it remains widely cultivated in Morocco (around 6,000 hectares); also in South Africa and to a much lesser extent in Italy, California and Chile. Australian vineyardists are aware of Cinsaut, which they call the 'black prince', but they rarely cultivate it. Overall, including plantings in Cyprus, Bulgaria, Romania, Russia, Portugal and the Lebanon, Cinsaut currently covers 45,000 hectares worldwide.

Colour and taste

Wines based on this grape variety are always moderately deep in colour. The addition of a certain proportion of Cinsaut makes blended wines more supple and harmonious by toning down such unwanted characteristics as high alcohol content in Grenache, or bitterness and concentrated tannins in the case of Carignan.

63

Clairette

This southern variety has a long association with the olive-growing regions of France. It extends from the north of the Drôme to the south of the Ardèche and yields a range of both still and sparkling wines.

Identifying the grape variety

Clairette has a felty white growing tip with a crimson border. The leaves are dark bluish-green in colour, orbicular, thick, contorted and bullate. They have five poorly defined lobes and an overlapping petiolar sinus. The grape bunches of Clairette are cylindrical-conical and winged. The grapes themselves are white with brown specks, ellipsoid and slightly pointed in shape with firm, juicy flesh.

Vineyard profile

Bud burst occurs late in this vigorous grape variety that performs well on impoverished soils. It is usually short-pruned to protect the fragile shoots from wind damage.

In France

Sales of white wines based on Clairette have slumped due to their tendency to rapid maderisation. For that reason, plantings have fallen steadily in the past 50 years from 14,128 hectares in 1958 to just 4,657 hectares in 1999. Previously sought after as an aperitif or as an accompaniment to game, Clairette wines were also used to make vermouth. These days, two appellations produce wines made exclusively from Clairette: Clairette-de-Bellegarde in the Gard and Clairette-du-Languedoc in the Hérault Valley. The latter produces a range of wines from dry (for drinking young) to liqueur and *rancio* (deliberately maderised) wines made from overripe grapes and matured in casks for three years. In the Drôme, Crémant-de-Die, a sparkling wine, is made exclusively from Clairette but Clairette-de-Die, also sparkling, is based predominantly on Muscat à Petits Grains and contains very little Clairette. Clairette blended with other white grape varieties is used to produce many AOC wines including: Châteauneuf-du-Pape, Côtes-du-Rhône, Cassis, Bandol, Côtes-de-Provence, Coteaux-d'Aix-en-Provence, Palette and Côtes-du-Ventoux.

Around the world

Clairette is not widely grown outside France except in South Africa where it accounts for more than 1,600 hectares of plantings and is used to make sparkling Vonkelwyn wines. It is also grown in Italy (where it is among the vines planted in the Nuragus di Cagliari vineyard in Sardinia), Morocco, Romania (for distillation), the Hunter Valley in Australia (where it is known as Blanquette), Uruguay, Israel and Algeria. In India, in the state of Karnataka, Clairette vines trained on pergolas produce large volumes of a mildly aromatic, agreeable wine. Total world plantings are in the region of 12,000 hectares.

Also known as ...

In the lower Rhône basin, Clairette vines are known as Clairette Blanche, Petite Clairette and Clairette Pounchudo (meaning pointed, due to grape shape). In Bandol in the Var, they are called Clairette Verte.

Colour and Taste

Dry Clairette wines, such as those from Bellegarde in the southeast of the Costières-de-Nîmes appellation, or those from the Languedoc, are light yellow in colour with hints of green. The characteristic bouquet is of white flowers with occasional notes of grapefruit and apple; the palate is low in acidity but finishes with the merest hint of refreshing bitterness.

Colombard

Despite its strong associations with Cognac and Armagnac, Colombard these days is not as popular as it once was with the *eaux-de-vie* producers who now prefer Ugni Blanc and Folle Blanche. And yet this Charentais grape variety once conquered the world, with plantings in California increasing dramatically during the 1970s and 1980s to rival those of Chardonnay.

Identifying the grape variety

Colombard has a felty white growing tip with a crimson border. The leaf is thick and orbicular, with a downy appearance and involute blade edges. The grape bunches are cylindrical in shape and winged and packed with golden-white ovoid grapes with juicy flesh.

Vineyard profile

Colombard is a moderately vigorous grape variety but it has the disadvantage of being susceptible to powdery mildew and grey rot. It therefore requires heavy pruning in the heart of winter when the wood is at its hardest. It does however have the advantage of being a very fertile plant, easily yielding 100 hectolitres per hectare. For producers back in the 1950s this was a point in its favour that outweighed the disadvantages.

Also known as...

In California and Texas, Colombard is known as French Colombard.

In France

Colombard was originally cultivated in the Charentes, in the Borderies, an argillaceous-chalky *terroir* northwest of Cognac, famous for the hazelnut bouquet of its *eaux-de-vie*. It was ideally suited to the production of Pineau de Charentes, a liqueur wine created from a blend of Charentais musts that was based on Colombard, Ugni Blanc, Montils and Sémillon and partially fermented with Cognac. Subsequently, Colombard spread to the southwest for the production of Armagnac and was grown as a secondary variety for use in white wine by the Bordeaux appellations of Côtes-de-Blaye, Côtes-de-Bourg, Entre-Deux-Mers and Ste-Foy-Bordeaux. Plantings of Colombard have fallen in France from 13,105 hectares in 1958 to 6,740 hectares in 1998 as large numbers of white grape varieties were uprooted in the Gironde following a slump in the sale of white wines. It remains of limited use in the Bordeaux appellations and in the Charentes, with the only increase in acreage being in Armagnac.

Around the world

Despite a slight fall in plantings, Colombard still accounts for 45,000 hectares worldwide. Almost half of these are in California which, despite its own uprooting programme, retains 18,633 hectares of Colombard for table wines and *eaux-de-vie*. There are also substantial plantings in Texas. Additionally, Colombard is grown in South Africa (where acreage has actually risen in recent decades), Australia, Mexico and Israel.

Taste

Colombard wines are reputedly better than those made from Folle Blanche, so long as production does not exceed 120 hectolitres per hectare. Above this level there is a significant loss of quality associated with green, coarse wines high in acid and low in alcohol. In the 17th century, cheap Colombard wines were popular with the Dutch who had replaced the English as the largest buyers of wines from southwest France. The wines were used to produce *eau ardente* (firewater), an *eau-de-vie* issued to ships' crews and exported throughout northern Europe. Under the right conditions, Colombard can yield not only quality base wines (responsible for the characteristic fruitiness in Armagnac, for instance) but also *vins de pays* with aromatic, youthful bouquets.

A vineyard in the Charentes, cradle of Colombard cultivation.

Gamay

Nearly 60 per cent of all Gamay vines in France are planted in Beaujolais, so the names Gamay and Beaujolais are very much linked in French viticulture. Things looked quite different in 1395 when Philip the Bold described Gamay as a *'très déloyalut plant'* (very disloyal plant) and banished it from the whole of the Côte d'Or. It found refuge in the thin, sandy *terroir* of Beaujolais.

Vineyard profile

Gamay bud burst occurs relatively early which exposes the vine to the risk of spring frosts. However, because it also ripens early, Gamay is widely cultivated in northern and mountainous vineyards. It is a moderately vigorous grape variety which, when short-pruned, produces from 60 hectolitres per hectare on the slopes to more than 200 hectolitres on low-lying ground. These profuse yields obtained on rich, fertile soils are the source of the poor quality wines that have damaged Gamay's reputation over the years. This was especially true after the bitter winter of 1709 when Gamay replaced Pinot Noir vines on the Ile-de-France.

In France

Gamay accounts for an impressive 36,700 hectares in France, and 99 per cent of all vineyard area in Beaujolais, so it is hardly surprising that it should have become known as 'Gamay Beaujolais'. It is the only grape used in the production of Beaujolais, Beaujolais-Villages and the 10 regional crus: St-Amour, Juliénas, Chénas, Moulin-à-Vent, Fleurie, Chiroubles, Morgon, Régnie, Côtes-de-Brouilly and Brouilly. These, and the Beaujolais-Villages appellations, are situated in the north of Beaujolais on poor, acid, granite or sandy terrain (known as *arène*) that brings out the best in the grapes. The more humble Beaujolais AOCs come from

the predominantly argillaceous limestone terrain in the south of Beaujolais. In Burgundy, Gamay is confined to two appellations: Bourgogne Grand Ordinaire, with the best wines being made from Gamay cultivated in the Yonne; and Bourgogne-Passe-Tout-Grain (blended with Pinot Noir), with two-thirds of production coming from Saône-et-Loire. Elsewhere in

France, Gamay is scattered around various regions producing wines sold *en primeur*. This applies to some Touraine wines from the Loire and some Gaillac wines from the southwest. Gamay also contributes to: agreeably fruity *vins de pays* such as the Jardin de la France wines; AOC wines such as the Coteaux-du-Vendômois; and the VDQS Côte-Roannaise

The rolling vineyards of Beaujolais are inextricably linked with Gamay: the most prestigious crus are situated in the north of the region, the more humble Beaujolais AOCs located in the south.

Auvergne wines (Côtes-d'Auvergne, St-Pourçain and Côtes-du-Forez) that are now considered as good as Beaujolais. Vineyards in the Aveyron, such as Estaign, Entraygues, Fel and Côtes-de-Millau, blend Gamay with Cabernet Franc, Cabernet Sauvignon, Syrah and Tannat producing full-bodied wines packed with fruit (blackcurrant and raspberries). Gamay is also the source of a range of rosés from appellations as diverse as the Loire and the Côte-Roannaise, as well as the pale-coloured rosés (*vins gris*) from Toul de la Moselle.

Around the world

In Europe, Gamay is widely cultivated in Switzerland, mainly in the canton of Valais where it is blended with Pinot to produce a celebrated regional wine called Dôle. In Geneva, it is used in place of local hybrids, and in the Vaud Gamay is generally associated with quality wines. It is also grown in Italian vineyards (in Val d'Aosta and Pérouse) as well as in Tuscany, Spain (in Aragona) and Portugal (in Trás-os-Montes). Additionally, there are a few plantings in Bulgaria, Hungary, Russia, former Yugoslavia, Slovenia, Romania and Luxembourg. Canada has some 50 hectares of Gamay, while in the United States the grape was for many years confused with a rather commonplace variety called Valdiguié, known to the Americans as Napa Gamay. There are also limited amounts of Gamay in South

Despite its steeply sloping vineyards Chiroubles, in the heart of a granite corrie (left), is the earliest ripening cru in Beaujolais. Below: the vineyards of St-Amour.

Opposite: Cru Morgon produces generous, full-bodied wines suitable for laying down for three to six years.

The Côte-Roannaise: wines to watch

Some 50 kilometres east of Beaujolais, Gamay is cultivated by *vignerons* in Roanne on the Monts de la Madelaine, the granite hillocks bordering the Massif Central mountain range. Côte-Roannaise wines are cherry-red with purple reflections and exuberant aromas of cherries, raspberries, blackcurrants, wild blackberries and strawberries. Depending on the period of tank fermentation (semi-carbonic maceration as in Beaujolais) and the age of the vines, the wines may be light, or robust and rustic, ready for drinking in winter following the harvest, or within three years of cellaring. This appellation also makes rosé wines with aromas of citrus, bananas, apples and pears.

Identifying the grape variety

Gamay has a downy white growing tip and the leaves are orbicular, slender and smooth. The blade is almost hairless, with a V-shaped petiolar sinus, three barely defined lobes and narrow teeth. The clusters are cylindrical, compact, sometimes with a small wing and densely packed with purple-black grapes thickly covered in bluish-white bloom. The flesh is juicy with a pleasant, if neutral flavour.

Africa, Australia, New Zealand and Israel. The total worldwide is around 40,000 hectares.

Colour and Taste

Gamay wines are usually rich, deep-red in colour with shades of violet; they are low in tannins but have good acidity. Thanks to the easy-drinking nature of Beaujolais wines, they soon became popular. Beaujolais was traditionally served in *pots du Beaujolais*, heavy-bottomed bottles containing 46 centilitres (about 3/4 pint), as an accompaniment to regional specialities based on *charcuterie* (cooked meats). In the 18th century, Beaujolais' reputation spread to neighbouring regions including the capital, thanks to the opening of the Briare Canal, and then further afield with the arrival of the railways. However things really took off in the

Also known as...

For many years Gamay was known as Gamay Noir à Jus Blanc to distinguish it from similar-sounding Teinturier vines. Elsewhere the name reflects the place of cultivation as in Gamay du Beaujolais, Gamay d'Auvergne, Gamay de Gien, Gamay de Toul and more. Other synonyms are Bourguignon Noir, Grosse Dôle or Gamay de la Dôle in the Valais, Switzerland, and Burgundi Kék in Hungary.

1950s with the launch of Beaujolais Nouveau, the 'newborn' wine that hits the shops the world over on the third Thursday of November. The secret lies in the process of semi-carbonic maceration used to vinify these aromatic, fruity grapes; they are macerated whole in vats for three to seven days. The wines taste of strawberries and raspberries with a slightly acidulous quality characteristic of *primeur* (newborn) wines. In addition to these carafe wines, Gamay also produces more distinguished crus capable of ageing for five years or more. These wines are deep ruby-red in colour with dark purple highlights. They combine fruity aromas and floral notes with a meaty, savoury palate supported by rounded tannins. This complexity is due not only to longer periods of tank fermentation but also to the granite *terroir* which suits Gamay better than the limestone terrain found in the south of the region.

Gewürztraminer

After Riesling, it would be hard to find a grape variety more characteristic of Alsace than Gewürztraminer. With its pretty bunches of ripe pink grapes, Gewürztraminer is the *gewürz* (spicy) variety of another pink variety called Traminer or Klevener de Heiligenstein. This non-perfumed grape is originally from the Italian Tyrol and was seen in Alsace in the 16th century. Both belong in a large family of vines related to Savagnin Blanc, these days cultivated in the Jura for the production of *vins jaunes* and other wines. Gewürztraminer or 'spicy Traminer' was first cultivated in Alsace in 1870 having been imported from vineyards in the Palatinate in Germany.

**Above: harvesting
in Riquewihr;
Top: Grand Cru
Sporen.**

Vineyard profile

Gewürztraminer is a vigorous, fairly early-ripening variety susceptible to frost and various diseases which in France rarely yields more than 50 hectolitres per hectare. German vineyardists in Baden have selected more productive clones although these are not necessarily of such good quality.

In France

Gewürztraminer plantings are increasing and currently stand at 2,676 hectares, mainly in Alsace and to a lesser extent in Moselle. Most consumers are familiar with the name Gewürztraminer because Alsace is one of the few French appellations to specify the grape variety on the label. Often used to produce dry wines, Gewürztraminer grapes that have been allowed to botrytise, or are picked when overripe, give distinctive sweet wines with excellent ageing potential.

Wines produced from late-ripening grapes have a minimum alcoholic content of 14.3 per cent abv while those produced from botrytised grapes (*sélection de grains nobles*) reach 16.4 per cent abv. Gewürztraminer is one of four grape varieties along with Riesling, Muscat and Pinot Gris permitted in the 50 Grands Crus of Alsace. While none of these tend to specialise in one particular grape, some favour certain varieties more than others. Gewürztraminer, for instance, does best on deep marls and limestone and reigns supreme in many of the vineyards along the *Route du Vin*, notably: Engelberg, Altenberg de Bergheim, Osterberg, Froehn, Sporen, Marckrain, Mambourg, Furstentum, Florimont, Goldert, Zinnkoepflé, Spiegel and Kessler.

Around the world

While plantings of Gewürztraminer worldwide are in the region of 8,000 hectares, the best-quality grapes come without question from Alsace. The USA has barely 1,000 hectares of Gewürztraminer in the states of California, Oregon, Washington and New York. Next comes Germany where Gewürztraminer accounts for just 1 per cent of planting in the Pfalz, Baden, Rhinehessen and Sachsen regions. Germany is followed by Austria (especially in Styria), Italy (in several northern provinces) and Spain (in Penedès). In eastern Europe Gewürztraminer is also associated with both sweet and dry wines. It gives good results in Hungary in the vineyards around Lake Balaton, and adds characteristic aromas to the sparkling wines of the Ukraine. Additionally there are limited plantings in Switzerland and

Luxembourg. In the New World, Gewürztraminer has been introduced in Canada, Argentina, Brazil, South Africa, Australia and New Zealand.

Colour and Taste

Gewürztraminer wines are immediately recognisable by their

golden hues tinged with peach due to the pigments in the ripe grapes and to the process of macerating the berries in their musts. The range of aromas in Gewürztraminer wines is equally distinctive, revealing an unmistakably spicy, exuberant bouquet of gingerbread and citrus peel mixed with hints of Muscat (such as roses) and exotic fruits (such as lychees). The palate is powerful and generous, echoing the range of aromas, often with additional notes of liquorice and smokiness. Late-harvested grapes yield the famous *vins de vendanges tardives* or *vins de séléction de grains nobles* (produced from late-harvested or botrytised grapes respectively) with characteristically opulent, flamboyant aromas. Notes of honey and apricots are especially noticeable in those wines produced from botrytised grapes.

Identifying the grape variety

Gewürztraminer has a felty white growing tip with a crimson border. The leaves are large, orbicular and crimped with revolute edges, five well-defined lobes and a totally closed petiolar sinus. The grape bunches are small, truncate and fairly loosely packed, with pink to light red ovoid grapes. The juice has a slightly musky flavour.

Opposite: Alsace is the only viticultural region in France to train the vines on very high supports so that the grapes catch the best sun.

Right: The Riquewihr vineyard, draped in a mantle of snow.

Also known as...

Gewürztraminer is known as Traminer in Germany, Traminer Aromatico in Italy, Tramini Piros in Hungary and Mala Dinka in Bulgaria. In Alsace it used to be called Savagnin Rose Aromatique and Gentil Rose Aromatique.

Grenache

Grenache, one of the great Mediterranean grape varieties, is at its best in vineyards on either side of the Pyrenees. It originated in Spain, probably in Aragon, and from the 12th to the 14th century spread from Roussillon in France to Sardinia in Italy.

Vineyard profile

Grenache bud burst occurs quite early on in the year with vines in France coming into blossom during the first week in June. They are usually short-pruned and have an upright growing habit thanks to vigorous shoots that can withstand drought and strong winds. Grenache nevertheless offers little resistance to disease so yields can be variable: from 20 hectolitres per hectare on impoverished slopes or when the crop is affected by *coulure*, to 60 or 80 hectolitres on rich soils – and even more when vines are planted on high ground.

In France

Grenache is grown in most Mediterranean AOCs in France including Châteauneuf-du-Pape, Côtes-du Rhône, Côtes-de-Provence and Coteaux-du-Languedoc. Plantings have increased steadily since the 1950s and now stand at 93,874 hectares (compared with 24,968 in 1958) spread between the vineyards of the Rhône Valley, Provence and Languedoc-Roussillon. Grenache is often blended with Syrah and Mourvèdre as well as Carignan for the production of dry red and rosé wines. The best are produced on the thin, warm pebbly soils characteristic of such appellations as Gigondas, Vacqueyras and Tavel, and are strong, with an alcoholic strength often more than 14 per cent abv.

Grenache also plays an important role in some famous *vins doux naturels* (sweet fortified wines) made from blends based predominantly or entirely on this grape. In Roussillon, for instance, and in a tiny part of Corbières, Grenache is used to produce the red Rivesaltes *vins doux naturels*. In vineyards close to the Spanish border and the Mediterranean, old Grenache vines clinging to schistous terraces are the secret of the

The Gigondas vineyards in the foothills of the celebrated Dentelles de Montmirail massif.

Demijohns of Maury wine.

legendary Banyuls. In a different landscape altogether, the steep schistous slopes north of the river Agly are the home of the Maury *vins doux naturels*.

Around the world

From Catalonia to Aragon, the Basque Country to Estremadura, Spain grows more than 104,000 hectares of Grenache. It is particularly significant in the wines of Rioja and Navarra. While Tempranillo is the most important grape variety in Rioja as a whole, Grenache dominates Rioja Baja, the 'low-Rioja' section of the region, which enjoys a hotter climate than Rioja Alavesa and Rioja Alta. Grenache grown in Rioja yields rich, full-bodied wines which can easily have an alcohol content of 15 per cent abv. In Navarra, Grenache accounts for 70 per cent of the area under vine, along with limited amounts of Tempranillo and Cabernet Sauvignon. In Italy, Grenache is planted in Sardinia (where it known as Cannonau), in Sicily and in Calabria. We also find Grenache growing in Greece,

Vin doux naturel : a rich fortified wine, obtained by adding alcohol in the form of grape spirit to the grapes during fermentation. This stops the fermentation process and retains sugar.

Rioja vineyards nestle in the valley of the river Ebro. Grenache is the dominant grape variety in Rioja Baja.

Vignerons in Banyuls have learned to tame nature and make do without mechanisation by building dry stone walls to hold up the steep, pebbly terraces.

Portugal (in the Ribatejo, the Estremadura, and the Alentejo) and on the island of Madeira. There are fairly substantial plantings of Grenache in Morocco, Tunisia, Argentina, California, Mexico and Australia. The world total is estimated to be around 240,000 hectares.

Colour and taste

Grenache grapes grown on pebbly, dry soils give generous, powerful, dry red wines with lovely golden-brown tones and aromas of red berries and spice. The tannins are rounded and well blended. The *vins doux naturels* are garnet-coloured or earthenware red, verging on mahogany after several decades of ageing. Vintage *vins doux naturels* (bottled immediately to seal in the fragrance) are steeped in aromas of cherries, blackcurrants, blackberries and Kirsch; those aged in contact with the air acquire hints of spice and burnt coffee, cocoa, dried figs and tobacco.

Banyuls

There are almost as many Banyuls as there are vineyards. *Rimage* Banyuls (the only vintages) are bottled at once to prevent ageing in contact with the air. Ordinary Banyuls and Banyuls Grand Cru are matured in large tuns or demijohns exposed on the roofs of the cellars, where the wines develop *rancio* characteristics (the nutty aroma, achieved by exposing the wine to oxygen and heat). They are then blended with other wines, and cellared for one year in the case of ordinary Banyuls and at least 30 months for Banyuls Grand Cru.

Identifying the grape variety

Grenache has a downy white growing tip with crimson traces. The leaves of this variety are a glossy light green in colour, cuneiform and smooth. They are thick, hairless and contorted, with five moderately well-defined lobes and a lyre-shaped petiolar sinus. The grape bunches are fairly large in size, truncate, compact and winged. The grapes are black and thick-skinned, with juicy, succulent flesh.

Also known as...

The Spanish name for Grenache is Garnacha but it also has regional names such as Aragonés in the area around Madrid, and Lladoner in Catalonia. In Sardinia it is known by the name of Cannonau, and in France the most common names for Grenache are Grenache Noir, Alicante, Roussillon and Rivesaltes. It is also called Tinto in the Vaucluse and Sans-Pareil in the Alpes-de-Haute-Provence.

Marsanne

This great white grape from the Rhône Valley, regularly paired with Roussanne, has shown steady progress since the 1990s thanks to new plantings further south in the country.

Vineyard profile

Marsanne is a vigorous grape variety associated with late bud burst and a drooping growing habit requiring short pruning. Despite its vulnerability to grey rot, powdery mildew and drying winds, Marsanne is generally more resistant, more flexible and more productive than its companion Roussanne, having an annual average yield of 50–60 hectolitres per hectare. This explains its growing popularity over the years, often at the expense of Roussanne.

In France

Marsanne accounts for 1,120 hectares of French vineyards and is the recommended grape variety throughout the *départements* of the Rhône and in vineyards south of Lyons as far as the Languedoc and Provence. The main area of concentration is the northern Rhône Valley, especially in the appellations of Hermitage, Crozes-Hermitage, St-Joseph and St-Péray – for a long time the

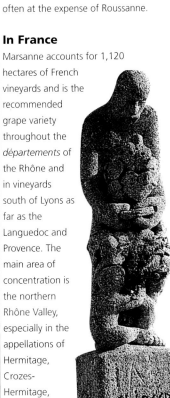

only areas in which Marsanne could be found. Marsanne is the dominant white grape variety in the Hermitage AOC; it far outranks Roussanne which only accounts for a small percentage of the blend. The vines cling to impressive sand and granite south-facing terraces on the left bank of the Rhône, concentrated in the vineyards of Méal and Rocoules. Syrah, meanwhile, makes up most of the plantings on the hillside of St-Joseph overlooked by the famous chapel. According to appellation rules, St-Joseph, Hermitage and Crozes-Hermitage may also add a proportion of Marsanne and Roussanne to their red wines (10–15 per cent), but this is rarely practised today.

Marsanne is much less common further south, with just a few plantings in the Coteaux-du-Tricastin and Vacqueyras. It is also found in Provence (in Cassis) but more in Languedoc-Roussillon which has adopted it as a subsidiary variety for blending with the regional white grapes.

Around the world

There are some 2,000 hectares of Marsanne planted worldwide. Switzerland grows it in the Valais where it is sometimes known as Ermitage. Swiss Marsanne can be harvested as late as mid-December, being vinified alone or blended with Pinot Gris to produce a sweet wine. Marsanne is also cultivated in Italy (where it is an authorised

variety in the province of Piacenza), in California and in Australia, principally in the Goulburn Valley in northeast Victoria, and in New South Wales.

Taste

Marsanne-based wines tend to be lighter, less fragrant and less delicate than those based on Roussanne. They are also low in acidity and therefore more inclined to rapid ageing. In France, as in Australia, the wines are sometimes matured in oak barrels. Marsanne grapes from Languedoc-Roussillon have more aromatic potential than Grenache Blanc and Macabeu but not enough to add distinctive aromas to blends. Marsanne is also used in the rich *vins de paille* (straw wines) produced in limited quantities only by the Hermitage AOC. These copper-coloured wines, with hints of crystallised fruits, are made from grapes that have been dried on straw-covered frames for at least 48 hours to concentrate the sugars (*passerillage*). In St-Péray, Marsanne produces still and sparkling pale-coloured wines, often tinged with green. With age, youthful aromas of hawthorn, violets and acacia give way to notes of honey and minerals. St-Péray sparkling wines have a vinosity distinct from other sparkling wines.

10 per cent of production in the St-Joseph appellation (in the northern Rhône Valley) is devoted to full, rounded white wines.

St-Joseph

These AOC wines are pale with green reflections in their youth, acquiring deeper tones of gold after several years of ageing. They have a delightful bouquet of hawthorn, fruits and honey and a beautifully rounded palate.

Identifying the grape variety

Marsanne has a felty white growing tip with a crimson border. The leaves are large, thick and extremely bullate with five deeply defined, often overlapping lobes and an overlapping petiolar sinus. The grape bunches are truncate, winged and fairly loosely packed with golden-white, juicy spherical grapes.

Also known as...

Marsanne is known as Ermitage in the Swiss canton of the Valais, White Hermitage in Australia and sometimes Rousseau in California. In St-Péray it is occasionally referred to as Roussette de St-Péray and in Savoie as Grosse Roussette or Marsanne Blanche.

Opposite: The low walls, or *cheys*, that support the terraces are a characteristic feature of the landscape in St-Joseph.

In St-Joseph (above), as in Hermitage (right), Marsanne is planted on granite terrain.

Mauzac

Mauzac originated in southwest France, probably in the region of Gaillac which remained the centre of its cultivation for many years. From there, wines were shipped to other areas via a network of waterways including the Tarn and the Garonne. It is likely, therefore, that the names Moissac, Moysac and Mozac are derived from the town of Moissac, an important centre of communication in the region. Mauzac could also have originated or spread from two other wine-producing communes, Mauzac in the Haute-Garonne and Meauzac in Tarn-et-Garonne.

The wines of Gaillac stand out in their originality thanks in part to the local grapes used, among them Mauzac, and in part to the range of styles offered: red, dry white, sweet white and sparkling.

Vineyard profile

Bud burst occurs late in this moderately vigorous grape variety. When goblet-pruned, Mauzac yields from 25–40 hectolitres per hectare on the slopes to more than 100 hectolitres in low-lying vineyards. It is fairly resistant to mildew and powdery mildew but very susceptible to outbreaks of grey rot, excoriose, grape moth larvae and mites.

In France

Plantings of Mauzac in France have decreased significantly in the past 30 years from 8,512 hectares in 1958 to just 3,350 hectares today. The main areas of cultivation are in the *départements* of the Tarn,

where many vines were uprooted, and the Aude where plantings of Mauzac are actually increasing. In the Tarn, Mauzac grapes are the source of the dry, sweet, slightly sparkling and sparkling Gaillac wines. In the Aude, they are the basis of the Limoux appellation wines of Blanquette-de-Limoux (90 per cent Mauzac blended with Chenin and Chardonnay), Limoux and Crémant-de-Limoux. *Vignerons* in Limoux traditionally planted Mauzac (nicknamed Blanquette because of the whitish down on the underside of the leaves) at the top of slopes where the thin soils became known as *blanquetières* (literally, 'producers of Blanquette'). Around 1530, the monks of the

Abbey of St-Hilaire used to harvest Mauzac at the end of October or beginning of November when the grapes were sweet enough to ferment slowly during the cool nights to come, and fermentation could be easily arrested. Once filtered, the wines were bottled in mid-fermentation. The following spring, the rise in temperature would trigger a secondary fermentation in most of the bottles, producing a wine high in sugar that still contained yeast deposits. Blanquette *méthode ancestrale*, which is in limited production today, is made by these ancient techniques. Blanquette-de-Limoux on the other hand is a *brut* (dry), medium-dry or sweet sparkling

85

wine made by the *méthode traditionnelle* (like Champagne). Mauzac these days is more usually planted on rich soils and productivity has risen accordingly (50 hectolitres per hectare). Grapes are harvested early in the morning at the end of September to obtain more acid musts and more enduring bubbles. In Gaillac, Mauzac is mainly planted on the hills of the right bank of the river Tarn alongside the local white grape varieties Len de l'El, Ondenc and Muscadelle. Conditions here produce loose bunches of Mauzac grapes that vary in colour from red to russet: these are regarded as the best quality grapes of the Gaillac appellation. Gaillac sparkling wines may be made by the *méthode artisanale* using residual natural grape sugars, or traditionally.

Around the world

Mauzac has not spread to vineyards outside France except for a few experimental plantings in Australia.

Taste

Mauzac is an aromatic grape giving wines with distinctive appley nuances on the nose. It is the basis of Blanquette-de-Limoux which mixes aromas typical of Mauzac with those of Chenin and Chardonnay: acacia and hawthorn followed by ripe fruits and notes of honey as the wine improves with age. Still Limoux wines, on the other hand, are more like Chardonnay, to which they owe their flesh and structure.

Gaillac

The white wines of Gaillac, dry or sweet, slightly sparkling or sparkling, are gold with delicate aromas of cooked apples and white peaches or pears, spices and honey. The dry wines are fresh; the sweet wines are noted for their richness. The sparkling wines, especially those made by the *méthode artisanale* (another name for *méthode ancestrale*, see page 85) are distinguished by their fruity structure.

Mauzac is the basis of Blanquette-de-Limoux, a sparkling wine proffering aromas of apples and flowers. Still Limoux wine is blended from Chenin and Chardonnay and aged in oak casks.

Identifying the grape variety

Mauzac has a felty white growing tip with a faint crimson border. The leaves of this variety are dark bluish-green in colour, small, thick and bullate with three barely defined lobes. The blade is slightly elongated and it is easily recognisable from the white downy tufts on its underside. The petiolar sinus is closed. The grape bunches are truncate-conical and compact, often with a small wing. The grapes are round, golden-yellow and thick-skinned with large pips.

Also known as...

Mauzac is often known as Blanquette in Limoux, and elsewhere by a variety of names based on alternative spellings such as Mausac, Moissac, Moysac, Mozac, Meauzac and Mansac.

Melon

This ancient Burgundian grape variety has abandoned its land of origin for the Loire Valley, where it is made into the light, fresh Muscadet wines from the Nantes region.

Compact, cylindrical bunches of Melon, with small, golden grapes.

Vineyard profile

Due to early bud burst, Melon is often affected by frost. It is also vulnerable to diseases such as mildew, powdery mildew and especially grey rot which nearly always develops on the grape bunches, so much so indeed that *vignerons* refer to Melon as *pourrisseux* (literally 'prone to rotting'). In some years, the grapes have to be harvested before they are completely ripe to prevent them from rotting. Melon is a moderately vigorous variety that regularly produces 40–50 hectolitres per hectare.

In France

These days, Melon is rarely cultivated in Burgundy where it accounts for just seven of the total 12,900 hectares in France. It remains, however, in the appellations of Mâcon Blanc and Crémant-de-Bourgogne. In the Middle Ages, Melon was so widespread in Franche-Comté that it attracted the wrath of Philippe II, King of Spain and Count of Burgundy, who on 1 December 1567 issued a royal decree 'forbidding on the advice of the government of his county, the planting and cultivating of new Gamez, Melons'. This decree did little or nothing to stop plantings, which from 1700 to 1731 were ordered for destruction once again by the parliaments of Burgundy and Franche-Comté. In a bid to save the threatened Melon, local *vignerons* chose to sacrifice its fiercest rival, Chardonnay, which they renamed Melon d'Arbois and which was destroyed in place of Melon.

Despite this, there are only two hectares of real Melon remaining in the Jura today, whereas Chardonnay is widely cultivated. In the Loire Valley, Melon was first planted in the Middle Ages in Anjou, where it was known as Petite Bourgogne, Petit Melon Musqué and Muscadet, while Chardonnay was known as Grande Bourgogne. It expanded into the Loire-Atlantique after the arctic winter of 1709. These days Melon is the only grape variety cultivated in the four Muscadet appellations of Muscadet, Muscadet des Coteaux de la Loire, Muscadet-Sèvre-et-Maine and Muscadet-Côtes-de-Grand-Lieu. It is also grown in the Vendée in the regions of Pissotte and Vix for the production of the white AOVDQS Fiefs Vendéens wines.

Around the world

Outside France, Melon is only really grown in any quantity in California, which has just 800 hectares devoted o it, mainly in the Napa Valley and in the counties of Sonoma and Monterey. Known as Pinot Blanc, American Melon is a high-yield vine producing wines quite different to those of France. Argentina also has around two hectares of Melon. The total worldwide is approximately 14,000 hectares.

Colour and Taste

Melon wines often remain in contact with the fine lees until bottling begins on 1 March in the year following the harvest. This produces very pale-coloured wines with an intense range of aromas and a beautifully supple texture.

Above: the vineyards of the Napa Valley in California.

Left: Fiefs-Vendéens vines planted in the foothills of the Massif Armoricain in the Vendée.

Opposite: Melon growing in the Pays Nantais.

Muscadet

These pale golden-green wines have a slightly sparkling quality when they are matured on the lees (*sur-lie*). Young Muscadet wine characteristically offers aromas of minerals and iodine, developing as the wine matures into notes of white flowers and citrus. Different appellations reflect a range of distinctive nuances such as the hints of musk detectable in a Muscadet-de-Sèvre-et-Maine. Muscadets are rounded, lively, moderately alcoholic wines (12 per cent abv). Those wines originating from the Atlantic coast are particularly memorable, thanks to a trace of bitterness at the finish.

Identifying the grape variety

Melon has a felty white growing tip with a crimson border. The leaf shape is orbicular and almost entire with revolute edges and a bullate surface. Grape bunches are cylindrical and compact; the grapes are small, spherical, golden-yellow and thick-skinned.

Also known as...

In the pays Nantais, Melon is often known as Muscadet or Petit Muscadet while in Anjou it is called Petite Bourgogne and Bourguignon Blanc. However, the Californians wrongly refer to Melon as Pinot Blanc.

Merlot

Little is known about the precise origins of this red grape from Bordeaux that is now cultivated worldwide. Prior to the 19th century, Merlot was regarded as a secondary grape variety known first as Crabutet Noir and later as Merlot or Vitraille. The presence of Merlot in the Médoc Grands Crus was first attested in 1857 by the ampelographer and then Minister of Agriculture, Victor Rendu.

Vineyard profile

Merlot bud burst occurs early, exposing the vine to the risk of frost. It is a fairly vigorous variety with a drooping growth habit that prefers cool terrain retaining sufficient moisture during the summer. Cultivation on very dry slopes leads to malformed bunches and small, stunted grapes. Merlot is particularly vulnerable to grey rot, powdery mildew, grape moth larvae and leafhoppers. It is also susceptible to *coulure* if the weather is unfavourable during flowering. In the event, yields may fall to 20–30 hectolitres per hectare, sometimes less. In Bordeaux, productivity generally varies from 40–60 hectolitres per hectare whereas in the Midi it can be as high as 80 hectolitres, producing wines with an alcoholic strength of 11 per cent abv. Yields of more than 100 hectolitres per hectare lead to significant loss of quality; thus the grape often called an 'improving' variety (one added to enhance a blend) can fail to live up to its name.

In France

In just a few years, Merlot has risen to become the No. 3 red grape variety in France after Carignan and Grenache. Plantings currently stand at 96,000 hectares thanks to new vineyards established in the Midi, although the main area for Merlot production is the Gironde, where there are just under 60,000 hectares. In the Médoc, Merlot vines grow at the foot of slopes on fresh, fairly argillaceous limestone soils, leaving the gravel mounds for Cabernet Sauvignon, which prefers a warmer terrain. Merlot in fact is more closely associated with the appellations of St-Emilion and Pomérol. The vineyards of St-Emilion are made up of Fronsadais molasse that is overlaid with argillaceous limestone and are situated on a plateau 60–90 m (198–297 ft) high, characterised by a hard rock cap of *calcaire à astéries* used by the village as building stone. In Pomerol all the vineyards have gravel terraces but where there is underlying clay, Merlot really shines. Thus in the Pétrus vineyard, for example, where the 'blister' of clay bulges through the thin gravel cover, 95 per cent of the area under vine is planted with Merlot, producing a range of generous, violet-scented wines. In Languedoc-Roussillon, Merlot acreage has boomed since the end of the 1960s, when Bordeaux grape varieties were classified as recommended throughout the south of France; Merlot now covers more than 23,460 hectares there. The red and rosé wines produced here are characteristic of grapes grown in a warmer climate but are of good quality in appellations such as Malepère and Cabardès, where the fierce heat is tempered by cooler Atlantic weather systems. Merlot vines remain limited in Provence, however.

Around the world

Merlot is widely cultivated by all the main wine-producing countries, from America to Australasia and South Africa to China, although its progression has been less rapid than that of Cabernet Sauvignon. Spain and Portugal make limited use of Merlot, but in Italy there are substantial plantings in the north as well as in Tuscany, and in Sardinia. Merlot accounts for 31,870 hectares of the area under vine in the DOCs of Trentino, Friuli and Veneto, where it gives satisfactory results when planted on slopes. In Switzerland, it is cultivated in the Ticino where soil and weather conditions favour the production of a premium wine called Val Mesoco. In eastern Europe Merlot is particularly prevalent in Slovenia (Istrie) and Croatia along the Dalmatian coast around Lake Ohrid. Merlot is also the No 2 grape variety in Bulgaria where it produces fairly meaty wines from the southern regions of Chirpan and Haskowo. Other countries on this side of the Atlantic that choose to cultivate Merlot are Russia, Moldavia, Romania and Hungary (in the Eger region and in the south of the country around Villany).
Across the Atlantic, there are just over 15,000 hectares of Merlot planted in California where it is sold as a single varietal, or is blended with Cabernet Sauvignon to produce Bordeaux-style wines.

It is also well established in Washington State, less so in the states of Oregon, New York and Virginia. Merlot is widely cultivated in Chile (where it is often confused with, or blended with Carmenère), in Argentina, South Africa and Australia. Merlot currently ranks seventh in the world league of grape varieties, accounting for more than 190,000 hectares.

Colour and Taste

Pure Merlot wines have a wonderful quality, as can be found in some of the Pomerol or St-Emilion crus wines where Merlot is the dominant grape variety. They have a much greater depth of colour than those based on other southern grape varieties and can be ready for drinking within two to three years. The wines offer delicious aromas of roasted berries and spices (and sometimes plums in the case of very ripe grapes). The current general infatuation with Merlot worldwide stems from the suppleness it imparts to wines blended with Cabernet Sauvignon, so making them ready for drinking earlier.

Pomerol

Despite its impressive ageing ability, Pomerol can also be enjoyed as a young wine, thanks to its supple, velvety tannins. Red with garnet reflections, this is a powerful, complex wine characterised by the aroma of violets that is the mark of Merlot, along with scents of red berries, leather and animal odours.

Opposite: The Swiss Ticino vineyards, with their terraced plots and almost Mediterranean climate.

Identifying the grape variety

Merlot has a felty white growing tip with a crimson border. The leaves are dark green, cuneiform and bullate with five well-defined lobes and pointed, narrow teeth. The petiolar sinus is lyre-shaped and the underside of the blade is cobwebby. The grape bunches, sometimes winged, are packed with blue-black spherical grapes that have moderately thick skin and juicy, pleasant-tasting pulp.

Also known as...

The Patois term for Merlot is Petit Merle. Other names include: Plant Médoc around Bazas; Sémillon Rouge or Semilhoun Rouge in the Médoc; Sème Dou Flube (*plant du fleuve* or river vine) in the south of Graves; and Bégney in Cadillac, Langon and St-Macaire.

Château L'Évangile in Pomerol, where 75 per cent of Merlot vines are planted on soils of clay and sandy gravel.

Mondeuse

This could be the vine of the Celtic Allobroges tribe referred to by Columelle and Pliny, but we will never know for sure. What we do know, however, is that this grape was traditionally cultivated in Savoie where it was the principal grape variety before the phylloxera epidemic. While plantings of Mondeuse these days are in decline in vineyards along the base of the Alpine flanks, it remains well-respected for the quality of its full-bodied red wines and is arousing new interest.

Identifying the grape variety

Mondeuse has a felty white growing tip and the leaves are contorted, delicately bullate and floppy. The blade is trilobate with revolute edges and the underside is cobwebby. The petiolar sinus is lyre-shaped and almost closed. The grape bunches are long and quite compact; the grapes are small, blue-black and juicy.

Vineyard profile

Mondeuse is a vigorous grape variety that is usually short-pruned in goblet form. Bud burst in this grape occurs relatively late, as does flowering. To ensure that the grapes ripen properly, the vines should be carefully planted on well-exposed slopes and production should be limited to 40–60 hectolitres per hectare. By contrast, Mondeuse that is planted on alluvial plains or valley bottoms produces more than 100 hectolitres per hectare, but the quality of the grape suffers. In Savoie, of which Arbin is one of the best-known crus, the grapes are ready for harvesting in the first fortnight of October, whereas in the Haute-Savoie they mature somewhat later on. Mondeuse is vulnerable to powdery mildew and mites.

In France

Plantings have been declining slowly in the past decades but Mondeuse is still present in the wines of the Vin de Savoie AOC and the Bugey VDQS. These days, Mondeuse covers just over 240 hectares, concentrated in a sharp, deep valley called the Combe de Savoie. On the right bank of the river Isère the southeast-facing slopes of the Cru Arbin along the Massif des Bauges are almost exclusively planted with Mondeuse. This is one of the three great Savoie classified growths, alongside Cruet and St-Jean-de-la-Porte. The Bugey vineyards, within the *département* of the Ain, are mainly planted on limestone rubble on the low-lying slopes of the Jura. Here Mondeuse shares the land with Poulsard Jurassien, and Gamay and Pinot Noir from Burgundy. Once substantial, the vineyards of Bugey today are now confined to isolated areas on the right bank of the Rhône as you face downstream.

Around the world

Mondeuse vines have been recorded in Australia (in the northeast of Victoria) and in Argentina. However the vines in question may have been wrongly confused with Refosco, as grown in Friuli, Italy. This variety has more sharply defined lobes than Mondeuse. Mondeuse is also known as Refosco in California, but this has nothing to do with the Italian variety.

Also known as ...

Black Mondeuse is known by a variety of synonyms of which the most notable are: Molette in Savoie; Gros Plant, Grant Chétuan and Meximieux in Bugey and in the Revermont.

Colour and Taste

Low-yield Mondeuse vines produce solid, deeply coloured wines with plenty of fullness and good ageing ability. Vin de Savoie is purple-red in colour with additional black cherry reflections when produced in the Cru Arbin. The bouquet releases aromas of strawberries, raspberries and blackcurrants, together with hints of violets and irises, and punctuated by nuances of spice. Slightly tough in youth, these wines acquire mellow tannins after two to six years of ageing.

Mourvèdre

Mourvèdre, also known as Morastell or Monastrell in Spain, is the second most important red grape variety in France. It has been grown in Provence since the 14th century, but how it came to be introduced from the Iberian peninsula remains a mystery. Rejected as unsuitable by *vignerons* in Provence when the vineyards were replanted after the phylloxera epidemic, Mourvèdre is now back in vogue, thanks to the excellent quality of its wines.

Vineyard profile

Due to its late bud burst, Mourvèdre is a valuable addition to vineyards on low-lying ground or mountainsides where there is a high risk of frost. In Provence, for example, it rarely shows any signs of life until early May. Mourvèdre is not without its faults, however. Slow to mature, its Spanish origins demand warm, well-exposed sites such as those in the vineyards of Bandol. For a long time, too, yields have been limited to 30 hectolitres per hectare but recent research launched in L'Espiguette and the Var seeks to introduce good-quality clones from the Spanish region of Murcia. Mourvèdre is prone to potassium deficiency, susceptible to mites and leafhoppers, and its roots are not frost resistant.

In France

Prior to the phylloxera epidemic Mourvèdre was the dominant grape variety in Provence where it reached as far as the Mées vineyards of Haute-Provence. Subsequently, when the vineyards were being replanted, Mourvèdre was found to graft badly onto the rootstocks available at the time, and was thus rejected by *vignerons* in favour of more productive varieties. Since 1960, the search for better quality vines has led to a spectacular increase in plantings of Mourvèdre, which have risen by more than ten-fold since 1958, from 618 hectares to the current figure of 7,300 hectares.

In Provence, Mourvèdre is planted in several AOCs including Cassis, the Côtes-de-Provence, the Coteaux-d'Aix-en-Provence, Palette and the Coteaux-Varois. It is at its most expressive, though, in the red and rosé wines of Bandol, accounting for at least 50 per cent of the red blends, alongside Grenache, Cinsaut, Syrah and Carignan as subsidiary varieties. Bandol is sheltered from the north wind by a vast amphitheatre of hills facing the Mediterranean, and the vines receive all the sun they need on long terraces of dried stone known as *restanques*.

Mourvèdre is one of numerous authorised grape varieties in the Rhône.

Mourvèdre vines flourish on the sunny terraced vineyards of Provence, especially in Bandol.

Around the world

Mourvèdre is one of the leading grape varieties in Spain, covering 73,870 hectares. It is found mainly in the eastern and central regions where it dominates the arid, limestone vineyards of Valencia, Almansa, Jumilla, Yecla and Alicante. Here, low-density plantings of ungrafted Mourvèdre produce robust wines high in alcohol. On the other side of the world, Australia has some 620 hectares of Mourvèdre (mainly in the Barossa Valley) while California has around 100 hectares. Russia, the Crimea, Azerbaijan and Uzbekistan also have a few hectares. The world total is around 85,000 hectares.

Colour and Taste

Mourvèdre produces a moderately potent (12 per cent abv), deeply coloured wine rich in tannins. Somewhat coarse and gamey in youth, it needs several years of ageing to mellow and develop distinctly peppery, fruity aromas of black-skinned fruits and spices.

In the Rhône Valley, Mourvèdre is one of 13 grape varieties authorised in the vineyards of Châteauneuf-du-Pape where it contributes complexity and good ageing ability when blended with Syrah and Grenache. It is also planted in the vineyards of the Côtes-du-Rhône, Côtes-du-Ventoux, Côtes-du-Luberon and the Coteaux-de-Pierrevert.

Mourvèdre is a more recent introduction in Languedoc-Roussillon where it is now regarded as an 'improver' variety and is regularly planted in appellations ranging from the Coteaux-du-Languedoc, Costières-de-Nîmes and Minervois to the Côtes-du-Roussillon and the steeply terraced vineyards of Collioure on the Mediterranean coast.

Opposite:
Low density plantings of Mou
the characteristically arid lime
terrain of Jumilla and Yecla in

Bandol

Red Bandol wines are rich ruby in colour and have an impressive tannic firmness that matures after some ten years of ageing. Their unique bouquet expresses aromas of red berries with notes of pepper, truffles, undergrowth and leather. Bandol rosé wines are just as fruity with a firmness capable of maturing for two to three years, thanks to the Mourvèdre element.

Identifying the grape variety

Mourvèdre has a felty white growing tip with a crimson border. The leaves are flat, lightly bullate, cuneiform-truncate and entire. The petiolar sinus is lyre-shaped and the underside of the blade is downy-pubescent. The grape bunches of Mourvèdre are conical, medium-sized and compact, sometimes with a small wing. The grapes themselves are small and black with thick skin densely coated in bloom, covering the soft, bitter-tasting flesh beneath.

Also known as...

In the Mediterranean, Mourvèdre is known by a variety of names, reflecting its many characteristics. In Provence it is called Mourvedon, Mourvès, Morvède and Négron due to the colour of its grapes, and Estrangle-Chien because of its bitter flesh. In the Drôme, its vertical shoots have earnt it the name Tire-Droit, or Espar or Spar in Hérault. Other names include Flouron or Flouroux due to the grapes' thick coating of bloom. The Spanish names for Mourvèdre are Morastell or Monastrell, while in California and Australia, as in the Pyrénées-Orientales, it is named after a town near Barcelona called Mataro.

Muscadelle

Muscadelle is found mainly in the Gironde and the Dordogne and is thought to have originated in Aquitaine. Although its grapes are delicately musk-scented when very ripe, Muscadelle is not related to any of the numerous Muscat varieties.

Vineyard profile

Muscadelle is a moderately vigorous grape variety characterised by late bud burst and annual yields rarely exceeding 50–80 hectolitres per hectare. At harvest time *vignerons* often have to remove grape bunches that have been spoiled by vinegar flies (Drosophila). Muscadelle is also susceptible to powdery mildew, grape moth larvae, wasps and especially to grey rot.

In France

Muscadelle is a recommended grape variety throughout the southwest and the Charentes, where it is planted in various AOCs, although never for vinification on its own. It is rarely replanted today and cultivation, which currently stands at just 2,080 hectares, is in decline. Muscadelle is blended with Sémillon and Sauvignon to produce the sweet wines of Bordeaux and the Périgord. It accounts for a small percentage of plantings, however, confined to either side of the Garonne, around its tributary with the Ciron, in the appellations of Cérons, Cadillac, Loupiac, Ste-Croix-du-Mont, Sauternes and Barsac. Some AOC vineyards, such as Château d'Yquem, plant no Muscadelle at all. As a result, the presence of Muscadelle is never as prominent as that of its blending companions in the *moelleux* (sweet) Dordogne wines such as Côtes-de-Montravel and Monbazillac.

Also known as...

Muscadelle is known by a variety of names that always reflect its subtly musky scent such as: Musquette, Muscadet Doux, Raisonotte and Angelico in the Gironde; Muscat Fou in Bergerac; Guilan Muscat or Guilan Musqué in the Lot, the Tarn and the Garonne; and Muscadelle in Bordeaux. Californians sometimes call it Sauvignon Vert, Uruguayans may refer to it as Sémillon and Australians still use the name Tokay because it was once confused with the Hungarian grape variety, Hàrslevelü.

Muscadelle is also used for the dry white wines of Entre-deux-Mers and Bergerac, but once again it is completely overshadowed by Sauvignon Blanc, with its elegant floral aromas.

Around the world

In Europe, there are limited plantings of Muscadelle in Hungary, Romania, the Ukraine, the Crimea and Russia for the production of table wines, dessert wines and grape juice. It is also grown in California and South Africa (where it is known as Muskadel) and more so in Australia, in the state of Victoria where it was for many years mistaken for Hàrslevelü, the Hungarian grape variety made into the unique sweet Tokay wine. Australian Muscadelle is used to make the liqueur Tokay, a popular

Identifying the grape variety
Muscadelle has a felty white growing tip and young, bronze-coloured leaves. The adult leaf is large, orbicular-reniform in shape, and bullate with three poorly defined lobes. The grape bunches themselves are also large, truncate and loosely packed with white to grey-pink grapes that become mottled as they start to ripen. The flavour of the grapes is similar to that of Muscat.

wine with the same concentration as Madeira. Altogether, some 5,000 hectares of Muscadelle have been planted worldwide.

Taste

Muscadelle wines are often very sweet with a distinctive perfume that is reminiscent of Muscat, but much more subtle.

Muscat blanc

Muscat is not a single grape variety but a vast dynasty of grapes all characterised by a powerfully aromatic bouquet. Of these, Muscat Blanc à Petits Grains is surely the most distinguished. Cultivation of Muscat in Mediterranean regions dates back to earliest antiquity when they were known as *Anathelicon moschaton* by the Greeks and *apianae* by the Romans after the bees and wasps that swarm around the sweet, musky grapes. The Romans were probably the first to plant Muscat in Gaul, in the province of Narbonne.

The Conservatoire Ampégraphique of Tressere allows researchers to study the aromas of Muscat planted on the pebbly soils of Rivesaltes.

Vineyard profile

Muscat Blanc has a vigorous, upright growing habit. Due to early bud burst with grapes maturing by the end of August in mainland France, it suits a range of climates and is planted as far north as Alsace. The disadvantages of Muscat are low resistance to pests and diseases, especially grape moth larvae and wasps. These can cause serious damage to the grapes, sucking out all the flesh to leave just the skin and pips. On thin, pebbly warm soils in France, Muscat Blanc yields no more than 28 hectolitres per hectare of must, to make *vins doux naturels*. Production can be twice as high on richer soils, but the grapes are neither as sweet nor as musky.

In France

Muscat Blanc is the star of the Muscat family accounting for 6,418 hectares in France. In the *département* of the Rhône, it is used in the ancient *vins doux naturels* of Frontignan, Lunel, Mireval and St-Jean-de-Minervois. Frontignan was already exporting Muscat wines in the reign of Charlemagne, their reputation growing as Montpellier became an increasingly important commercial centre in the 12th century. By the 20th century, these vines were being exported at very high prices to Germany, Holland and England. The vineyards of Muscat de Frontignan are spread around the southeast-facing flanks of the

Muscat Blanc
vines in
Frontignan.

The stark,
dazzlingly white
limestone soils of
St-Jean-du-
Minervois.

Muscat-de-St-Jean-de-Minervois

This pale Muscat wine offers wonderfully exotic aromas of lemongrass, lychees and passion fruit. The palate is laciness itself, remarkably long with an opulence that is balanced by the freshness of the bouquet. These Muscats owe their unique character to the fact that the grapes are picked later on in the year than in other appellations, the cooler climate encouraging a leisurely rate of sugar concentration and the more gradual development of the aromas.

Massif de la Gardiole, protected from the north winds giving favourable conditions for ripening. Old Muscat vines are planted on dry, pebbly soils unsuitable for all other forms of cultivation but excellent for soaking up the heat during the day to keep the vines warm at night. A few kilometres to the east, the Muscat vineyards are open to the sea on the argillaceous-limestone soils of Mireval, as on the gentle, rubble-covered slopes of Lunel. Here, the maritime humidity tempers the fierce summer heat, encouraging a leisurely rate of sugar concentration in the grapes and the gradual development of the aromas. St-Jean-de-Minervois lies on the western borders of Hérault at the foot of the southern slopes of the Montagne Noire. The vines here

Identifying the grape variety

Muscat Blanc has a felty white growing tip with a crimson border. The young leaves are glossy and bronze-coloured, becoming orbicular in shape with a thick, crimped texture. They have five moderately well-defined lobes that overlap at the top of the blade and pointed, narrow teeth. The petiolar sinus is closed with parallel edges. The grape bunches are long, cylindrical and rarely winged forming a compact mass of amber-yellow, spherical grapes with thick skin that becomes spotted with rust when the grapes are completely ripe. The flesh is firm, juicy and very sweet, with a musky fragrance.

are planted on a brilliant white limestone plateau, where poor, shallow soils produce a wine of lacy substance with perfectly balanced freshness and sweetness. In Provence, the equally spectacular vineyards of Beaumes-de-Venise, overlooked by the Dentelles de Montmirail, produce a refined, fruity white Muscat. The vineyards of Cassis and Roquevaire near Marseilles also used to produce Muscat wines that were partly blended with Mourvèdre. Vineyards in the Pyrénées-Orientales produce sweet wines from a blend of Muscat Blanc and Muscat d'Alexandrie, the latter of

Also known as...

This legendary Mediterranean grape variety is known by many synonyms that reflect either its botanical characteristics or the *terroir* on which it is grown. In France it is known as Muscat Blanc à Petits Grains, Muscat de Frontignan, Muscat de Lunel, Muscat de Die, Muscat d'Alsace or Muscat Blanc du Valais. Elsewhere in the Mediterranean, its names include: Moschato Aspro and Moscatofilo in Greece; Moscatel de Grano Menudo or Moscatel Fino in Spain; Moscatel de Bago Miudo or Moscatel Branco in Portugal; and Moscata Bianca, Moscatello Bianco, Moscato di Canelli, Moscato d'Asti and Moscato Bianco Commune in Italy. In northern Europe, it is called Weisser Muskateller in Germany and Tamîioasa Romaneasca in Romania. In English-speaking countries it is known as Brown Muscat or White Frontignac in Australia, White Muscadel in South Africa and White Frontignan in England.

The vineyards of Constantia, in Cape Province, South Africa.

Opposite: In Piedmont, Italy, Muscat Blanc is used to make Moscato d'Asti, the lightly sparkling wine with fresh, grape-like aromas.

which has increased in popularity since the mid-20th century. Its advantages are that it is less attractive to birds and insects, more productive and its grapes can be made into wine (as they are now) or eaten as table grapes. Its disadvantages are that it ripens later on and requires a warm climate to completely express itself. Thus within the vast Muscat-de-Rivesaltes AOC, which extends for some 4,500 hectares from Corbières to the Pyrenees and Canigou to the Mediterranean, it is the pebbly terraces of Rivesaltes that produce the most complex Muscat d'Alexandrie. Outside mainland France, the most recent of the Corsican appellations, Muscat-du-Cap-Corse, produces a wine worthy of Muscat Blanc from grapes planted on mainly

schistous soils bordered by rocks and the maquis. The wine combines a velvety palate with the crisp, fresh taste of table grapes. While often associated with sweet wines, Muscat Blanc is also used to produce other types of wine. Grapes from the slopes of the middle valley of the Drôme are blended with Clairette to produce one of the oldest wines in the world, Clairette-de-Die, a sparkling wine made by the *méthode ancestrale* (see page 85) based on secondary bottle fermentation using only residual grape sugars. In Alsace, the AOC dry wine Alsace-Muscat was traditionally based on Muscat Blanc, although this is now increasingly replaced by Muscat Ottonel.

Around the world

Italy is the second most important country for Muscat Blanc after France, with 13,530 hectares. In the temperate Piedmont region, Muscat Blanc, grown on gently sloping vineyards above the Tanaro and Bormida rivers, yields such celebrated sparkling wines as Moscato d'Asti and Asti Spumante. In southern Sicily, Muscat Blanc is planted on hot, arid terrain to give liqueur wines such as Moscato di Noto and Moscato di Siracusa. Greece is renowned for the quality of its Muscat wines, particularly the island of Samos, where Muscat Blanc is planted on terraces at an altitude of 800 metres (2,640 ft). Patras and Cephalonia in the Peloponnese produce Muscat wines of a similar standard, 80 per cent of which are exported.

While Muscat Blanc exists in the Iberian peninsula, it is not as widely planted as Muscat d'Alexandrie. Moving in a circle from southeast Europe to the north, Muscat is popular in Turkey, Austria, Romania and southern Russia. Germany grows a small amount of Muscat Blanc in Baden-Württemberg, where it is blended with red Muscat grapes and Muscat Ottonel, but only on a limited scale. In the New World, Muscat Blanc is grown in California, in particular in the San Joaquin Valley, south of Central Valley where the AVA (Approved Viticultural Area)

Madera is well known for its sweet wines. Muscat Blanc can also be found in Argentina and Brazil. In Australia (in northeast Victoria), Muscat Blanc produces a dark liqueur wine called Liqueur Muscat. In South Africa, Muscat Blanc à Petits Grains was the source of the legendary wine of Constantia produced at the end of the 18th century. It continues to be well established in Cape Province, imparting a distinctive fragrance to other liqueur wines. Plantings of Muscat across the world amount to approximately 45,000 hectares.

Taste

Muscat Blanc-based wines are immediately recognisable by their aromas of roses and rosewood, due to the naturally occurring terpenic compounds in the grapes. These aromas are often described as musky. In *vins doux naturels*, they are accompanied by hints of fruit (grapes, dried apricots, pink grapefruit, exotic fruits, lychees) and flowers (roses, white flowers) and lemongrass. The palate should not be excessively sweet and heavy but subtly balanced by the fresh aromas. Dry wines made from Muscat Blanc often finish with a distinctive bitterness.

Muscat ottonel

Muscat Ottonel is the fruit of a seed that was first planted by a nurseryman from Angers called Robert Moreau in the mid-1800s. The origins of this grape variety are not entirely clear although it is believed to be descended from Chasselas and Muscat de Saumur. Its botanical characteristics are unmistakably those of Chasselas – young reddish leaves, very long tendrils, round leaves – while its musky perfume resembles Muscat de Saumur

Identifying the grape variety
Muscat Ottonel has a cobwebby growing tip. Its young leaves are vivid red becoming orbicular, smooth and contorted with five defined lobes. The petiolar sinus is shaped like a narrow lyre and sometimes overlaps. The grape bunches are cylindrical and quite loosely packed with spherical, medium-sized, pale yellow grapes with a delicate musky flavour.

Vineyard profile

Muscat Ottonel, propagated after 1852, was originally grown as a table grape. It then became a wine grape in Alsace, replacing Muscat Blanc which matured too late for such a northerly region – the grapes failed to ripen properly in some years. In fact, Muscat Blanc and Muscat Ottonel are rarely planted in the same vineyard plot, but in plots judged by *vignerons* to suit the respective habits of each variety of grape. Muscat Ottonel needs plenty of warmth during flowering to ensure proper setting of the fruit. It prefers deep, moist soils that are low in limestone. It is vulnerable to attacks of downy mildew, powdery mildew and rot, and is also susceptible to *coulure* which in some years can wipe out the entire crop. As a result, the productivity is variable with yields fluctuating between 50 and 100 hectolitres per hectare.

In France

Muscat Ottonel accounts for some 158 hectares of vineyards in the Haut-Rhin and the Bas-Rhin, in Alsace. It can be vinified alone for the production of Alsace-Muscat, but is more usually blended with Muscat Blanc and Muscat Rose à Petits Grains, the coloured variety of Muscat à Petits Grains, which is now quite rare. Muscat Ottonel is one of the great Alsace grape varieties, formally recognised by the 50 Grands Crus. It contributes to the reputation of the Hatschbourg vineyard, where it is more widely planted than Riesling. Muscat Ottonel can also be vinified as sweet wines made from *vendanges tardives* or *grains nobles* (late-harvest or botrytised) grapes, although these types of wine are more often based on Pinot Gris, Gewürztraminer, and Riesling.

Around the world

Unlike Alsace, which prefers to use Muscat Ottonel for the production of dry wines, eastern and central European countries use it to make sweet wines. This is the case in Austria, in Burgenland and the Wachau; Hungary around Lake Balaton; and Romania in the Tirnave region. Muscat Ottonel is also grown in Moldavia, the Ukraine, Germany (but only on a limited scale), Canada and South Africa. There are some 2,000 hectares planted worldwide.

Also known as...
Muscat Ottonel is called Muskat Ottonel in Germany and Austria, in the former Czechoslovakia and Slovenia. The Hungarians call it Ottonel Muskotály and the Romanians know it as Tamîioasa Ottonel or Muscat de Craciunel Tîrnave. In South Africa it is known mainly as Muscadel Ottonel.

Taste

Muscat Ottonel imparts a sense of roundness to Alsace-Muscat whereas Muscat Blanc produces wines of a more forceful, solid structure. Alsatian *vignerons* are not concerned solely with the production of sweet Muscat wines from overripe or botrytised grapes. They also want to preserve all the freshness and intensity of the grape in dry wines to be drunk as aperitifs, with a first course (Alsace-Muscat is one of those rare wines that goes well with asparagus, for instance) or with *kouglof* – an Alsace brioche studded with raisins. These golden-green wines have distinctively musky tones with aromas of budding blackcurrant that develop with age into more spicy flavours, sometimes with hints of liquorice.

Négrette

Négrette adds character to the red and rosé wines of the Frontonnais (the area between Toulouse and Montauban) and, a little further north, to the wines of Lavilledieu, an ancient wine region once owned by the order of the knights of St John of Jerusalem.

Identifying the grape variety
Négrette has a felty white growing tip with a crimson border. The leaves are cuneiform and lightly bullate with five moderately well-defined lobes and narrow, pointed teeth. The petiolar sinus is V-shaped and more or less narrow, and the underside of the blade is slightly downy. The grape bunches themselves are small, cylindrical and winged, forming a compact mass of black, spherical or slightly ovoid grapes with succulent flesh.

Vineyard profile

Négrette is a fertile, high-quality grape variety that is characterised by late bud burst, low productivity when planted on argillaceous-limestone soils and a high incidence of *coulure* on alluviums. It prefers extremely poor soils of gravel, stony silt and clay (known as *boulbenc*). Low resistance to powdery mildew and grey rot has sadly led to a decline in its cultivation.

In France

Following a slight decrease in plantings, Négrette now covers just 1,330 hectares of French vineyards, principally in the Côtes-du-Frontonnais AOC and the VDQS area of Lavilledieu. It is particularly well suited to the iron-rich soils of Fronton. In the early 20th century,

The vineyards of the Côtes-du-Frontonnais retained Négrette, one of their original grape varieties, when the vineyards were replanted by the co-operatives of Fronton and Villaudric.

after the ravages of phylloxera, Négrette fell seriously out of favour with *vignerons* owing to the failure of its scions when grafted onto the rootstocks available at the time. The frosts of 1956 did much to restore its reputation, however. Today, it shares terraces in the Tarn with Cabernet Franc, Cabernet Sauvignon, Côt, Mérille and Syrah. To the north of Frontonnais, Négrette grows alongside Cabernet Franc, Gamay, Syrah and Tannat on terraces in the Tarn and the Garonne. It covers 30 per cent of the small wine region of Lavilledieu, where it is planted in siliceous alluviums and gravel.

Also known as ...
In France, Négrette has several synonyms, each acknowledging the dark black colour of the grapes. In the Gers it is known as Négret de Gaillac or Négret du Tarn, Morillon, Mourelet, Chalosse Noir or Vesparo Noir; in Charente it is called Petit Noir. In California, it is known as Pinot St-Georges.

Around the world

California retains some 80 hectares of Négrette, which for many years was known by the name of Pinot St-Georges in the United States and was not accurately identified as Négrette until 1980.

Taste

If the people of Toulouse have discovered their ideal wine in Côtes-du-Frontonnais, it is thanks to Négrette, which gives these wines their ruby colours and delicious aromas of violets, red berries and liquorice. Red wines based predominantly on Négrette typically offer up the scents of the original *terroir* on which the grapes were grown, and can usually age for five years. The red and rosé wines of Lavilledieu are rounded and fruity. In former times, Négrette also produced the best red wine of the Charente.

Ondenc

Ondenc, with its poetic, southern-sounding name, has grapes bursting with light-coloured juice, described in French as *ondoyant* (rippling) and *aqueux* (watery). Though it is something of a curiosity these days, Ondenc deserves to be rediscovered.

Identifying the vine

Ondenc has a felty white growing tip with a crimson border. The leaves are orbicular and lightly bullate with five well-defined lobes and slightly revolute edges. The petiolar sinus is a narrow lyre shape and the underside of the blade is downy. The teeth are broad and not very prominent. The grape bunches are truncate and densely packed with ellipsoid, juicy grapes that are yellowish-white in colour.

Vineyard profile

Bud burst occurs early in this rather bushy vine. Yields are invariably low as Ondenc vines are highly susceptible to viral infections; they are also affected by powdery mildew and rot. Cultivation has steadily declined over the years as *vignerons* have moved over to less vulnerable vines.

In France

Ondenc is part of the viticultural heritage of southwest France where it now accounts for just four hectares. No longer in vogue, Ondenc is nevertheless authorised in various appellations including Bordeaux, Bergerac, Montravel and the Côtes-de-Duras. In Gaillac, Ondenc can still be found growing on the limestone slopes of the right bank of the Tarn although *vignerons* now prefer Mauzac,

Also known as…

There are many variations on the name Oudenc, depending on the local patois (such as Oundenc, Onden, Doundent or Ondainc). It is occasionally called Blanquette or Blanquette Sucrée in the Gironde and the Bergerac region; Primaï or Primard in Fronton and Villaudric due to its early grapes; Dourec(h) in the Jurançon; and Gaillac in southwest Gers. In Australia it goes by the names Blanc Select, Irvine's White and Sercial.

Le Len de l'El, Muscadelle, Sémillon and other Sauvignon varieties. In Cahuzac-sur-Vère, a winegrower called Robert Plageoles has set out to revive ancient Gaillac grape varieties, including Ondenc, which he uses to make Gaillac Doux. This sweet wine is produced exclusively from Ondenc grapes that have dried out on the vine in the southerly winds, or have developed noble rot. Gaillac Doux is a particular rarity since Ondenc is hardly ever vinified alone.

Around the world

There are nearly 300 hectares of Ondenc in Victoria, Australia, where it has various names. Portugal and California used to grow Ondenc at the start of the 20th century but no longer do so today.

Taste

Ondenc produces moderately alcoholic wines with a delicate bouquet. Gaillac Doux, made from raisined grapes, has aromas of figs, apricots, angelica, quince and honey.

Pruning the vines in the Très-Cantous domain in Gaillac, owned by Robert Plageoles.

Petit manseng

The Pyrénées-Atlantiques *département* is the home of Petit Manseng, a white grape variety with thick-skinned grapes which are susceptible to noble rot in the vineyards of Jurançon. This variety has become increasingly popular with *vignerons* in the past 50 years for the quality and distinctive characteristics of the wines it produces.

Jurançon

Jurançon is a wine of regal and literary legend. It is said that drops of Jurançon were rubbed on the lips of the future Henri IV at his christening; Colette wrote, 'As an adolescent, I became acquainted with a passionate, arrogant prince as treacherous as any great seducer: Jurançon wine'. This golden *moelleux* (sweet) wine has many aromas, including honey, spices, white flowers and crystallised fruits. It is lively and generous, concentrated yet delicate on the palate.

Vineyard profile

Petit Manseng is a vigorous grape variety that is characterised by early bud burst and a preference for a deep, pebbly terrain. The shoots must be long-pruned, staking the vines individually at a height of 1.70m (5ft 6in). Constant treatments are needed to protect Petit Manseng from outbreaks of powdery mildew. It is also prone to downy mildew and, to a lesser degree, black and grey rot. Yields are dependable but very low (15–25 hectolitres per hectare); harvests are carried out in batches once the grapes are botrytised. In addition to noble rot, the thick-skinned berries are also susceptible to *passerillage* (the drying out of the berries on their stalks to concentrate the sugars). It is not uncommon for harvesting to continue beyond the first snowfalls.

Identifying the grape variety

Petit Manseng has a felty white growing tip with a crimson border. The leaves are dark green, orbicular and delicately bullate with three to five moderately well-defined lobes. The petiolar sinus is U-shaped and the underside of the blade is cobwebby. The grape bunches are truncate and winged; grapes are small, white and spherical with thick skin.

In France

The reputation of the famous *moelleux* (sweet) wines of the Jurançon is founded on Petit Manseng. The vines are planted alongside Courbu and Gros Manseng in vineyards facing the magnificent Pyrenees. Petit Manseng is also grown in the appellations of Béarn, Irouléguy and Pacherenc-du-Vic-Bilh. Plantings in France have increased by nearly twenty-fold in the past 60 years, from around 30 hectares in 1950 to 570 hectares today.

Around the world

Today, there are around 1,000 hectares of Petit Manseng in Uruguay, where it was first planted in the 19th century by the Basque vineyardist settlers.

Also known as ...

There are many ways to spell Petit Manseng including Petit Mansene, Mansenc Blanc, Mausenc Blanc, Manseing and even Mansic. In the Basque country, it is known as Ichiriota Zuria Tipia.

Taste

Grapes that are naturally high in sugar are the key to the sweet Jurançon wines that can have an alcoholic strength of between 12 and 16 per cent abv. These are wines of good acidity, a certain refinement, possessing a distinctive bouquet. In particular, Jurançon wines reflect the influence of Petit Manseng, which imparts overtones of ripe fruits (peaches, citrus fruits) and spice (cinnamon), exotic fruits and loquats.

Traditionally trained up fruit trees, Petit Manseng vines today are fastened to tall stakes (*hautains*) to protect them from frost.

Pinot noir

Pinot Noir is *the* grape responsible for the fine red wines of Burgundy, and has spread to the French vineyards in the north of Champagne and Alsace. It was undoubtedly grown in Gaul long before the Roman conquests and would have been recorded by the Latin agronomist Columelle. Today, Pinot Noir is planted in vineyards the world over.

Vineyard profile

Pinot Noir is a somewhat temperamental grape variety that is sensitive to many diseases. Early bud burst makes it particularly vulnerable to spring frosts, and in northern vineyards it should never be planted on low-lying ground or at the foot of slopes. Damp argillaceous terrain should also be avoided as cold, wet weather during flowering increases the risk of *coulure* and *millerandage*. Yields also vary, depending heavily on the region in which it is being grown. In a bid to overcome these drawbacks, scientists have created a variety of clones. In Champagne, for instance, *vignerons* choose clones that are more productive for that area than those favoured in Burgundy.

In France

Because it ripens early, Pinot Noir is planted in all the great vineyards of northern France and central Europe. Its wines have satisfied the appetites of kings, princes and

other notables, as well as the monastic orders who founded the classified growths, most of which are still in existence today. In 1999, Pinot Noir accounted for 25,870 hectares of the total area under vine in France, which represents a three-fold increase since 1959. The main areas of concentration are in Burgundy, Champagne, Alsace and the Loire Valley. In Burgundy, Pinot Noir expresses a range of characteristics depending on the *terroir*. Grapes with the most complex bouquet come from an area extending nearly 50 kilometres (31 miles) from Dijon to Dezize-lès-Maranges on the Côte d'Or. Marsannay marks the beginning of the Côte-des-Nuits, a succession of 29 appellations renowned for the

finesse of their wines. They include such names as Gevrey-Chambertin, Morey-St-Denis, Nuits-St-Georges, Chambolle-Musigny and Vosny-Romanée. The most firmly structured of the Burgundy wines come from Pinot Noir that is planted on soils rich in limestone marls, in the Premier Cru and Grands Crus vineyards of Grands-Echézeaux, Romanée, Romanée-Conti, Romanée-St-Vivant, Chambertin, Clos de la Roche, Musigny and Clos du Vougeot. Further along, at the northern end of the Côte de Beaune, deep soils give rise to the full-bodied wines of Corton and Savigny-lès-Beaune. The central area is home to such stars as the Beaune Premiers Crus, Pommard and Volnay.

Above:
Pinot Noir takes
up over a third of
vineyard acreage
in Champagne.

Right:
the vineyards of
Chambertin and
Chambertin-Clos-
de-Bèze, on gentle
east-facing slopes
between the
woods and the
Route des Grands
Crus, **where**
limestone soils
allow Pinot Noir
to express itself
perfectly.

Continuing south to the Côte Chalonnaise, Pinot Noir is planted alongside Chardonnay in the appellations of Mercurey, Givry and even Rully, producing agreeable red wines which have a good ageing ability. Further along, in the Mâconnais, Pinot Noir is used exclusively for the production of regional Burgundy wines, gradually making way for Gamay, which increasingly dominates the vineyards from here to Beaujolais further south.

In the north of the country, the sparkling wines of Champagne are based predominantly on Pinot Noir. Here, the grapes are picked by hand and placed gently in little baskets. They are then taken as quickly as possible to the winery for crushing to prevent the skins from colouring the juice. Pinot Noir can be vinified alone or blended with Pinot Meunier to produce Blanc de Noirs champagnes. Pinot Noir wines can also be blended with various proportions of Chardonnay. While the resulting Champagnes have very different organoleptic properties, the fruity aromas of Pinot Noir are always apparent. This ancient grape variety also leaves its mark on the still red wines of Champagne. The most famous are the Coteaux Champenois from the communes of Bouzy, Ambonnay and Ay, where the vineyards are well exposed to the sun. Pinot Noir is also the source of a unique rosé wine from the commune of Les Riceys. Here, only the oldest vines, planted in selected vineyard plots, are capable of producing the very ripe, sweet vintages required for this unique wine that was well-respected at the court of Louis XIV.

In Alsace, Pinot Noir performs best on the limestone soils of the sub-Vosgian Hills. Here, the preferred grape varieties are not Pinot Noir, but Riesling, Gewürztraminer, Pinot Gris and Muscat. Local *vignerons* nevertheless make the most of its distinctive qualities, thanks to improved methods of vinification (designed for maximum extraction of constituents) and ageing in oak. In addition to rosé wines, Pinot Noir also yields fruity red wines capable of moderate ageing. Last, but by no means least, the famous Crémant d'Alsace is also based on Pinot Noir. Various appellations throughout the Loire Valley list Pinot Noir among their red grape varieties, among them Sancerre, Menetou-Salon, Touraine Rosé, Crémant-de-la-Loire and several regional VDQS areas. In the Jura, Pinot Noir – or Gros Noirien as it is known locally – is used to make red Côtes du Trousseau and the sparkling Crémant du Jura. In the Ain, the Bugey vineyards grow Pinot Noir as a subsidiary variety to Mondeuse Savoyarde and Gamay.

Romanée-Conti

This archetypal Pinot Noir is capable of infinite development and should be allowed to age for at least ten, if not twenty years or more. With age, the colour takes on a beautiful crimson hue and the bouquet presents delightful aromas of blackberries, cherry stones, violets, truffles and even spices. When tasting, it is found to be supple, elegant and intense on the palate.

Opposite:

The walled vineyard of Clos de Vougeot was founded by the monks of Cîteaux Abbey in the early 12th century and is still in production nowadays. It encloses around 50 hectares of Pinot Noir.

Identifying the grape variety

Pinot Noir has a felty white growing tip. The leaves are dark green, orbicular and medium-sized. They are thick and coarsely bullate with three barely distinguished lobes and a narrow lyre-shaped petiolar sinus. In the autumn, the leaves become a lovely shade of yellow, more or less mottled with red. The grape bunches are small, cylindrical and occasionally winged, with a very hard peduncle. The grapes cluster together and are round, blue-black or dark purple, densely coated with bloom. Their skin is thick and richly pigmented and the flesh is scant but succulent.

Also known as...

In the 14th century, the poet Eustache Deschamps referred to Pinot Noir as Pynos in his *Ballade de la Verdure des Vins.* These days its many names include: Noirien, Pinot Fin and Plant Fin on the Côte d'Or; Morillon Noir in the Loir-et-Cher; Orléans, Plant Noble in Touraine; Plant Doré in Champagne; Gros Noirien in the Jura and Switzerland, where *vignerons* also use the names Cortaillod and Klevner. In Germany, it is named Blauer Burgunder and Spätburgunder; in eastern Europe it is called Burgundi Crni in Slovenia and Croatia, and Burgundi Mic in Romania.

Until 1945 the Romanée-Conti vineyard cultivated ungrafted vines injected with carbon sulphate to protect them from phylloxera. These days the vineyard has been replanted with vines that are descended from original Romanée-Conti stock.

Around the world

Pinot Noir is widespread throughout eastern Europe for the production of premium red or sparkling wines. Germany is its second home with 7,600 hectares, known locally as Spätburgunder. German winegrowers have rediscovered its potential and some use Pinot Noir to produce a sweet wine made from late-harvested grapes. Baden accounts for two-thirds of German Pinot Noir acreage, followed by the Pfalz, Rheinhessen, Württemberg and the Rheingau. In Switzerland, Pinot Noir is grown mainly in the German cantons, with limited plantings in Neuchâtel, where it is the only authorised red grape variety, and in the Valais, where it is blended with Gamay to produce the celebrated Dôle. In southern Europe, Pinot Noir has been successfully adapted for cultivation in the coolest parts of Italy (in Trentino-Alto Adige and Friuli) and Spain (in Aragon, Catalonia and Valencia).

Pinot Noir is also planted in the most northern viticultural areas of Europe. There are 45 hectares of Pinot Noir in England, which is remarkable in a country where the production of red wine is limited due to the cool, damp climate. But this intrepid traveller does not stop there. On the other side of the Atlantic, various microclimates favour the expression of Pinot Noir,

especially in the United States, in Oregon and California. The Los Carneros vineyard in California, with its cool, misty climate, owes its reputation to full-bodied red and sparkling wines based on Pinot Noir. Further south, Pinot Noir is increasingly grown in the irrigated vineyards of Argentina and Chile. The greatest change of all has been in South Africa, New Zealand and Australia where plantings of Pinot Noir have increased substantially with promising results. In all, there are some 60,000 hectares of Pinot Noir worldwide.

Colour and Taste

Pinot Noir wines are usually rich in colour but with little depth except for certain darker-coloured wines that are produced from clones. Their sustained, complex aromas linger on the palate, youthful scents of red and black berries developing with age into flavours of cherries in *eau-de-vie*, game and leather. The alcohol content ranges between 10 and 12 per cent abv on average. Thanks to their silky, well-blended tannins, Pinot Noir wines have an average ageing capacity of five to ten years depending on the cru. In exceptional vintages, wines from some of the top crus can continue to mature in the bottle for several decades. After many years of ageing, these ruby wines take on pale rosé tones that eventually discolour the bottle. The best Pinot Noir wines come from grapes grown on limestone and marl soils in exclusively temperate climates. In southern regions, the grapes actually ripen during the hottest period, yielding wines that are certainly alcoholic but lack distinctive aromas. Thus, in hot countries only vineyards planted at altitude can produce grapes of acceptable quality.

Opposite: The
Nierstein vineyard
in Rheinhessen,
nestling in a
meander of the
river Rhine.

Pinot Noir
performs
exceptionally well
here, in the cool,
misty climate of
Los Carneros in
California.

Below:
Baden (with the
Durbach vineyard
shown below) is
the centre of
Pinot Noir
cultivation in
Germany.

Poulsard

This ancient grape variety was acknowledged in Franche-Comté as far back as 1386 under the name of Polozard. Today it is used to make the varied red and rosé Jura wines as well as the astonishing *vins de paille* (also known as *vins jaunes*) of the region.

The *vins de paille* of the Jura

These wines, blended from Poulsard, Chardonnay and Savagnin, are the signature wines of the Jura region. The grapes are left to dry naturally on straw-covered frames until January, before they are pressed and given long periods of fermentation. After three years' maturation, including eighteen months in wooden caskets, these unique *vins jaunes* are the colour of old gold and as smooth as velvet, with the subtle aromas of dried and crystallised fruits.

Vineyard profile

Poulsard bud burst occurs early, exposing this delicate grape variety to the risk of spring frosts. Poulsard is a low-yield vine lacking in vigour and prone to *coulure* in cold, wet weather. It is also susceptible to downy mildew, powdery mildew and grey rot. While delicious to eat, the grapes are not easy to market as table grapes as their thin skins are easily damaged in transit.

In France

There are just over 300 hectares of Poulsard grown in mainland France, principally in the Jura, the Ain and the Doubs. It is also planted in the Arbois and Côtes-du-Jura appellations, where it is made into both red and light, aromatic rosé wines. It also does particularly well on the marly soils of the Pupillin commune.

Identifying the grape variety

Poulsard has a white, cobwebby growing tip with a crimson border. The young leaves are first bronze-coloured, turning blue-green with five deep lobes, and narrow teeth. The petiolar sinus is U-shaped and more or less open. The blade surface may be smooth or coarsely bullate in texture with pubescent veins on a hairless underside. Grape bunches are rounded and winged, and the blue-black grapes are ellipsoid, thin-skinned and fleshy.

In the Etoile AOC, Poulsard is blended with Chardonnay and Savagnin for still and sparkling white wines. In the Bugey VDQS, Poulsard is planted on gentle slopes in the ridges of the Jura and is used in the sparkling wines of Cerdon.

Colour and Taste

Red Poulsard wines are usually described as being a pale red or deep pink in colour. The rather pale

Also known as...

Poulsard, also known as Pelossard, Ploussard and Pleusard, is so named because the colour of its grapes resembles that of wild sloes, or *pelosses* in Patois. In the Revermont it is called Mescle or Mècle, which in Ain patois means 'mixture' and refers to the indeterminate colour of the berries.

colour of the young wine deepens with age to acquire delicate rosé tones. While it is often vinified alone, Poulsard is also blended with Trousseau and Pinot Noir. The first combination adds structure, the second adds colour, and both add a wide range of fruity aromas. The wines are never aged in wood for more than a year, in keeping with the style of *clairet* (deep pink) wines that are very low in tannins and as refreshing as a rosé. Poulsard is vinified as a white wine in the Etoile AOC, a method which provides a pleasantly rounded palate with aromatic finesse.

Poulsard vines endure the rigours of a continental climate in the Côtes-du-Jura vineyards, which punctuate the fields and forests of the region.

Riesling

The fine wines of the Rhine, Mosel and Alsace owe their reputation to this great noble grape variety. Probably cultivated in Germany during Roman times, it is believed to have been introduced to Alsace in the 9th century.

The south-facing Alsace Grand Cru Muenchberg in the Bas-Rhin is almost exclusively planted with Riesling.

Vineyard profile

Due to late bud burst and late ripening, Riesling demands sunny, well-exposed slopes in northern vineyards. The grapes may be ready for picking by mid-October but, to avoid delays in ripening, the vines should be planted on fairly thin, pebbly soils. Riesling offers good resistance to the frequent winter frosts in Alsace and Germany.

In France

With the exception of a few plantings in the Languedoc, around Aigues-Mortes, Riesling is planted only in Alsace, where it accounts for more than 20 per cent of the vineyard area. At the start of the third millennium there were 3,400 hectares of Riesling in France, a figure which continues to grow. Riesling thrives on southeast-facing granite and sandy soils (arènes) where the grapes develop pleasant floral aromas as well as mineral nuances that emerge with age. It excels in the renowned sites of Alsace, especially in the Bas-Rhin vineyards, such as Altenberg de Wolxheim, and notably those of Kaselberg and Wiebelsberg, where it is the only grape used. In the Haut-Rhin, it is planted on higher ground at Schlossberg, and on the steep south-facing slopes of Sommerberg. Riesling is the dominant grape variety in the vineyards of Brand and Pfingstberg, on the sandstone soils of Kitterlé, the sandy marls of Saering and the volcanic bedrock of the Rangen de Thann. One of four Alsatian grape varieties (with Gewürztraminer, Pinot Gris and Muscat) it is used for *vendanges tardives* (late-harvest) and *sélection de grains nobles* wines (made from botrytised grapes). The latter are relatively rare, however, as Riesling grapes are too thick-skinned to favour the development of noble rot. Moreover, while over-ripening changes the expression of Pinot Gris and Gewürztraminer, it has little effect on Riesling.

Around the world

The home of Riesling is Germany, where it is the leading white grape variety, accounting for 23,000 hectares. It is grown mainly on terraces in the valleys of the river Rhine and its tributaries, the Mosel, the Nahe and the Neckar, which reflect the sun's rays onto the vines. The centres of Riesling cultivation are Mosel-Saar-Ruwer, the Pfalz and, in particular, the Rheingau, where Riesling represents 90 per cent of the vineyard area. The wines produced can be dry, sweet

(*Auslese, Beerenauslese* and *Trockenbeerenauslese*) or made from grapes frozen on their stalks: the famous *Eiswein* or ice-wines. In the heart of the Saar, to the east of the village of Wiltzingen, producer Egon Müller grows Riesling grapes of matchless intensity on the steep slopes of the Scharzhofberg Hill. Conditions here favour ripening despite the harsh weather, making this one of the rare *terroirs* in the Saar capable of producing Beerenauslesen (wines made from late-harvested grapes). Elsewhere in Europe, Riesling is grown in Switzerland, in the Valais; in Austria, in the Wachau; in

Above: The Scharzhofberg Hill in Mosel-Saar-Ruwer overlooks the village of Wiltzingen. Riesling is planted on 11 hectares of steep, schistous soils in closely spaced rows at a density of 8,000 vines per hectare.

Above: The celebrated Schloss Johannisberg in Rheingau, where Riesling has reigned supreme since 1720.

Schloss Johannisberg

The renowned Schloss Johannisberg vineyard, formerly owned by Metternich, is planted on slopes overlooking the river Rhine. This vineyard is so much a symbol of Riesling that the vine is now commonly referred to as Johannisberg. Legend has it that in the autumn of 1775 Schloss Johannisberg unwittingly discovered the potential for botrytised grapes to make sweet wines by vinifying Riesling grapes affected by noble rot. Today, the 40-hectare vineyard is entirely planted with Riesling, yielding wines of perfectly balanced richness and acidity.

various eastern European countries; in the Ukraine; and in Russia where it is made into sparkling wines. It has also proved more or less successful in New World sites such as the elevated vineyards of Clare Valley and Eden Valley in South Australia where strongly alcoholic wines are produced. However, the cool New Zealand climate produces more elegant Riesling wines. In the Americas, Riesling is most widespread in the United States (in California and Washington State); and in Canada (in British Colombia and Ontario). Here, Riesling is associated with good-quality dry wines and ice-wines. It is also cultivated in several South American countries, including

Identifying the grape variety

Riesling has a greenish-white downy growing tip. Young leaves are cobwebby and yellowish in colour with a bronze hue, becoming orbicular, thick and coarsely bullate. The petiolar sinus usually has parallel or overlapping edges and the leaf's underside is cobwebby-pubescent. Grape bunches are almost cylindrical with a short, woody peduncle. Grapes are small and spherical, forming a compact mass of attractive light green to golden-yellow, thick-skinned grapes that are flecked with reddish-brown spots when ripe, and have a delicately aromatic flavour.

Argentina. South Africa is the latest country to have introduced Riesling. Additionally, vineyards all over the world make and market fake Riesling wines based on grape varieties that are mistaken for Riesling proper. Riesling Italico, which is grown throughout the Balkans and the former Yugoslavia, is a prime example of this. Others are the Australian Clare Riesling and Californian Grey Riesling.

Taste

Riesling offers a range of distinctive aromas. These are particularly intense when the grapes are grown on the slate schists and argillaceous

Also known as...

In Alsace, Riesling is sometimes known as Riesling Rhénan and Gentil Aromatique. The Germans, meanwhile, call it Rhein Riesling or Johannisberg, and the Swiss call it Petit Rhin.

soils of the Mosel and Rheingau. Riesling generally produces dry wines with the capacity to mature slowly over periods of ten years or more. Typical Riesling aromas include refreshing citrus notes that are mixed with scents of flowers, crystallised fruits, peaches and lime blossom. Grapes grown on granite soils have mineral nuances that develop into petrol-like aromas with age. On the palate, the acid structure can support these rich aromas, ensuring elegant, rounded dry wines. The acid also helps to balance the sweetness of wines produced from late-harvested and nobly rotted grapes.

German Rieslings are less alcoholic and livelier than their Alsatian cousins, although this is offset by their intense fruitiness. This vivacity also safeguards the elegance of the *moelleux* (sweet) wines.

Roussanne

This grape variety from the Rhône Valley is difficult to cultivate and has not always been popular with winegrowers. However, thanks to the intense, elegant aromas it can offer, it is now arousing new interest as a quality grape.

Chignin-Bergeron (Vin de Savoie)

Though unusually fresh for a Rhône Valley wine that is based on Roussanne, Chignin-Bergeron is quite high in alcohol with an agreeably sweet palate. The wines are produced from grapes that are harvested in batches, and reveal the delicious aromas of crystallised and dried fruits, and figs.

Vineyard profile

Roussanne is characterised by late bud burst and low, sometimes irregular yields, never exceeding 40–50 hectolitres per hectare. This particular variety matures rather late for the Rhône Valley and is sensitive to powdery mildew and grey rot.

In France

Plantings of Roussanne are increasing in mainland France: they have risen from just 10 hectares in 1958 to 676 hectares 40 years later. Roussanne is grown in the Rhône appellations of Hermitage and Croze-Hermitage, St-Péray, St-Joseph, Châteauneuf-du-Pape and the Côtes-du-Rhône. Conditions are ideal for Roussanne on the pebbly terraces of Hermitage, overlaid with alluviums around Rocoules and Méal. Though it generally represents a small percentage of blends, it is the signature grape in some cuvées produced by Hermitage

Identifying the grape variety

Roussanne has a felty white growing tip with a crimson border. The leaves are large, orbicular and rather thick, appearing bullate and contorted. The petiolar sinus is lyre-shaped and overlapping and the underside of the blade is pubescent. The grape bunches are cylindrical and compact. Grapes are small and spherical, changing from golden-white to reddish-brown when ripe, and containing little juice.

Roussanne excels in Savoie, on the slopes of Chignin.

and Crozes-Hermitage. In St-Joseph, Marsanne and Roussanne account for just 10 per cent of the vines, and these are concentrated between Châteaubourg and St-Jean-de-Muzols, the historic part of the appellation. Both varieties are also

Also known as...

Roussanne is highly regarded in Savoie, where it is known as Bergeron.

grown in the granite *arènes* of St-Péray, where Roussanne contributes to blends of still wines and is occasionally vinified alone. Further south Roussanne is blended with Grenache Blanc and Clairette, adding intense aromas to Châteauneuf-du-Pape wines. In Savoie, the Chignin cru at the foot of Les Bauges produces some remarkable white wines that are known as Chignin-Bergeron and based on Roussanne (known locally as Bergeron).

Around the world

Roussanne is recommended in Italy in the Tuscan province of Lucques where, together with Trebbiano, it comes under the Montecarlo DOC. There are also a few plantings of Roussanne in California and Australia (in Victoria).

Taste

Roussanne can produce elegant wines with fragrant aromas of honey, apricots and hawthorn. Thanks to its good acidity Roussanne can also improve the ageing capacity of blended wines.

Sauvignon blanc

Sauvignon Blanc, now cultivated all over the world, was originally famous as the white grape variety of Bordeaux and the Loire Valley. It is the source of great sweet wines and intensely fragrant dry whites, and is much sought after in vineyards throughout France – in short, it is a grape variety of unmistakable character.

Vineyard profile

This grape variety, originally from Bordeaux, is characterised by a vigorous growth habit, medium bud burst and low fertility. In fact, excessive vigour or physiological disorders frequently result in a failure to set fruit (*coulure*), although better quality, more productive clones yield 50 –100 hectolitres per hectare. Sauvignon Blanc is sensitive to a number of diseases, including powdery mildew and grey rot.

In France

Plantings of Sauvignon Blanc in France are steadily increasing, having risen from 5,500 hectares in 1958 to more than 19,970 in 1998. In the Bordeaux area and southwest France, Sauvignon is blended with Sémillon and Muscadelle to produce the great sweet AOC wines of Sauternes, Barsac, Loupiac, Ste-Croix-du-Mont, Bergerac and Monbazillac; it is also used in a few dry white wines such as Bergerac. In the Loire Valley, Sauvignon vinified alone as a dry wine is particularly aromatic when cultivated in the areas of Pouilly-Fumé, Sancerre, Quincy and Reuilly. It also plays a part in the wines of Haut-Poitou and several *vins de pays*, especially in the Charentes. In Burgundy, Sauvignon grown in

The vineyards of Sancerre extend along slopes of *terre blanche* (white earth), hard limestone and flinty clays facing the Loire.

the Auxerre vineyards gives a light, agreeable, dry white wine called Sauvignon-de-St-Bris, the only other Burgundy with Bourgogne-Aligoté to be named after a grape variety. Sauvignon was first introduced here at the start of the 20th century, in the wake of the phylloxera epidemic. In the south of France, Sauvignon can be found in Bandol and Cassis. Meanwhile plantings have soared in the Languedoc for the production of Vins de Pays d'Oc.

Around the world

Like the other classic French grape varieties, Sauvignon Blanc is now firmly established in almost every winemaking country, and accounts for almost 45,000 hectares worldwide. In Italy, Sauvignon Blanc is mainly concentrated in the provinces of Vicenza in Veneto and Parma in Emilia-Romagna, as well as in the regions of Friuli and Alto Adige. In Spain, it is established in the Penedès and is authorised for cultivation in Catalonia and Castilla-León. Sauvignon can also be found in Portugal – in the Douro and especially the Minho – and in other European countries.

In the United States, Sauvignon is present in California and additionally in the states of Oregon, Washington, New York and Georgia. Sauvignon's success is largely due to the Californian producer, Robert Mondavi, who in 1970 was much acclaimed for his dry wine, Fumé Blanc, made from Sauvignon aged in oak.

There are also plantings of Sauvignon in Canada, Mexico, Chile, Argentina, Brazil, Uruguay and Bolivia. In many American countries, however, the official figures for Sauvignon acreage are inaccurate because of ampelographical errors. This is the case in Chile and Argentina, where Sauvignonasse was for many years known as Sauvignon. Similarly, in California, authentic Sauvignon (which was sometimes known as Savagnin Musqué) was planted alongside Sauvignon Vert, which was, in fact, Muscadelle. In addition to Cyprus and Israel, Sauvignon is

also successfully grown in South Africa, Australia and New Zealand. The last has cemented its reputation in the wine world, thanks to its wonderfully fruity, lightly sparkling Sauvignon wines. Those originating from Marlborough in the north of South Island now rank as some of the finest wines in the world.

Taste

Good, true Sauvignon aromas should suggest box tree and crushed blackcurrant buds – not the wild odours of cat's urine so often cited as typical, but which are more characteristic of wines created from under-ripe Sauvignon grapes. Surprisingly, for wines with such complex bouquets, the grapes are odourless. The aromas open out and develop during fermentation but they are not enhanced further by a short period on lees or maturation in the bottle. Sauvignon wines from the Loire wines are pale gold in colour with distinctive notes of blackcurrant buds coupled with more complex scents of flowers and lemony white fruits. On the palate the lively aromas are coupled with a supple texture.

In sweet Bordeaux wines, a small percentage of Sauvignon adds freshness to balance the warmth of the botrytized Sémillon grapes. Sauternes dessert wines are also blended from Sémillon, plus 10–20 per cent Sauvignon.

Sancerre

In Sancerre, Sauvignon grapes express different aromas depending on the terrain on which they were grown. Grapes from the *terre blanches* and limestone marls have a characteristic bouquet of narcissus; those from the hard limestone *caillottes* reveal notes of blackcurrant and box; those from flinty clays offer nuances of broom and flint. On the palate, *terre blanches* wines are firm, developing their aromas gradually; *caillotte* wines are lighter and more elegant; wines from flinty clays are firmer.

Identifying the grape variety

Sauvignon Blanc has a felty white growing tip with a crimson border. The young leaves are downy and yellowish in colour with a bronze hue. They develop into small orbicular leaves with a contorted, almost curly, appearance and a coarsely bullate texture. The five lobes are sharply defined, the petiolar sinus is lyre-shaped and open, and the underside of the blade is downy. Sauvignon Blanc's grape bunches are also small, truncate, compact and sometimes winged. The grapes themselves are small and ovoid, turning a lovely golden-yellow colour when fully ripe. They are thick-skinned with soft flesh similar in taste to Muscat.

Also known as...

In France, Sauvignon Blanc, is known as Blanc Fumé or Fumé in the Nièvre, and sometimes Surin in the Loir-et-Cher. In Australia and California, it is known as Blanc Fumé and Sauvignon Blanc. Other names include: Feigentraube (fig grapes) in Germany; Muskat Sylvaner in Austria; Muskatani Silvanec in Croatia and Slovenia; and Gros Sauvignon in Russia.

Opposite: The village of St-Bris-le-Vineux in the heart of the Auxerre region, home of Sauvignon-de-St-Bris, a masterful wine that closely resembles wine from the Loire. Right: The nearby vineyards of Sancerre.

Sémillon

Sémillon remains the second most widely cultivated white grape variety in France after Ugni Blanc, although acreage is steadily decreasing. Traditionally from the Gironde, Sémillon has spread throughout southwest France, where it plays a leading role in all the great white appellation wines of the region.

Vineyard profile

This Bordeaux variety is vigorous and productive. Bud burst is long, with the vine continuing to produce buds after the risk of spring frosts has passed. Sémillon, moreover, offers good resistance to *coulure*, downy and powdery mildew, although it is sensitive to grey rot in wet years. *Vignerons* take steps to limit yields to ensure premium grapes with high sugar content. This is particularly important in Sauternes, where production relies on Sémillon.

In France

In 1999, there were just 14,446 hectares of Sémillon compared with 35,993 hectares in 1958. Despite this, it is still the predominant grape in the great sweet wines of Bordeaux: Sauternes-Barsac, Ste-Croix-du-Mont, Loupiac, Cérons and Cadillac. Misty mornings and sunny afternoons encourage the development of noble rot (*Botrytis cinerea*), shrivelling the thick-skinned grapes and concentrating the sugars. The fungus also significantly reduces the crop (to less than 20 hectolitres per hectare), which is harvested in successive batches as the grapes attain the ideal 'shrivelled' condition. Sémillon (blended with Sauvignon Blanc and Muscadelle) is also the source of dry white or *moelleux* (sweet) wines and the sparkling Crémant-de-Bordeaux. In the Dordogne, Sémillon is the predominant grape variety in Bergerac, where it produces the sweet wines of Monbazillac and Saussignac, as well as dry wines combining fruity aromas with an elegant body.

Around the world

There are close to 34,000 hectares of Sémillon worldwide, mainly in the New World and much less in Europe. It is especially popular in Chile and Argentina for the production of dry wines; likewise in the United States, in California and Washington State.

Sémillon (known locally as Wyndruif, or wine vine) remains important in South Africa, where it was once the leading white grape variety. In Australia, plantings of Sémillon are concentrated in the Hunter Valley in New South Wales, where it yields excellent dry wines with the capacity to age for 10 years or more.

Botrytis cinerea, or noble rot, shrivels up the grapes, so concentrating the sugars.

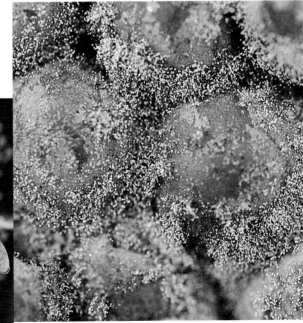

Above: Château Dudon in the Ciron region, whose micro-climate featuring morning mists gives rise to the great Barsac wines.
Right: The 12th century church of Loupiac, a commune without a village, sits amid the vines.

Taste

The characteristic aromas of Sémillon are more discreet and less acid than those of its blending companion, Sauvignon Blanc. Nevertheless, after a few years of ageing, wines based on Sémillon develop unmistakable notes of honey, beeswax and dried fruits, combined with a richly rounded palate that balances the freshness of the Sauvignon. Because high yields spoil the quality of Sémillon, productivity of more than 50 hectolitres per hectare is associated with lower quality wines.

Sauternes

With age, the distinctive golden tones of young Sauternes wines acquire an almost amber hue. The nose has characteristically 'roasted' nuances of noble rot mingled with aromas of almonds, hazelnuts, honey, apricots, ripe pears and acacia flowers. The palate presents a perfect balance of sweetness and freshness, with no trace of heaviness.

Identifying the grape variety

Sémillon has a felty white growing tip with a crimson border. The young leaves of this variety are downy and yellowish with bronze-coloured irregularities. The mature blade is orbicular, contorted and thick with a cobwebby underside, five sharply defined lobes and an open lyre-shaped petiolar sinus. The grape bunches of Semillon are cylindrical and winged, forming a compact mass of spherical, golden-white grapes that turn pinkish when fully ripe. They are thick-skinned and juicy with a lightly musky flavour.

Also known as...

Sémillon is sometimes known as Sémillon Muscat in Sauternes, or Sémillon Roux and Gros Sémillon in the Gironde. South African vineyardists call it Greengrape, due to its bright green leaves. In Australia it is sometimes called Hunter River Riesling, although this is also the local name for Chenin.

Château d'Yquem, home of the most magical of all the Sauternes wines, thanks to a microclimate that tends to favour premium quality grapes and the policy of the Lur-Saluces family to limit yields to just one glass of Yquem per vine.

Sylvaner

Widely cultivated in Germany and Alsace, Sylvaner is generally thought to be of Austrian origin. According to some ampelographers however, it is native to Transylvania, hence its synonyms Sylvanertraube, Salvaner and Sylvaner.

Vineyard profile

Sylvaner is a vigorous grape variety that is characterised by early bud burst and reliable fertility. Average yields for long-pruned vines planted on slopes are 60–80 hectolitres per hectare rising to more than 150 hectolitres for vines planted in low-lying vineyards. As a result, Sylvaner was traditionally used to make table wines. Sylvaner is not particularly resistant to spring frosts and the canes are at risk from winter frosts. Additionally, Sylvaner foliage is sensitive to disease.

In France

Sylvaner plantings have fallen slightly in mainland France to 2,065 hectares. It is confined to Alsace, where it was introduced in the 17th century and is an authorised variety for the Alsace appellation. More common in the Bas-Rhin than in the Haut-Rhin, Sylvaner is traditionally associated with the light, fresh wines of the Barr region. However, vines that are planted in favourably exposed deep soils can also yield more complex wines. While Sylvaner is not authorised for Alsace Grand Crus, it does give particularly convincing results in the vineyards of Zotzenberg in Mittelbergheim. In the Haut-Rhin, the Cru Zinkoepflé also produces respectable wines based on Sylvaner.

Around the world

Before 1960, Sylvaner was the No 1 grape variety in Germany (with

Identifying the grape variety

Sylvaner has a felty white growing tip with a crimson border. The young leaves are downy and yellowish in colour, becoming nearly rounded, smooth or lightly bullate and contorted. The blade may be entire or composed of three barely distinguishable lobes and the underside is hairless. The petiolar sinus is closed or shaped like a narrow lyre. The grape bunches are cylindrical or slightly conical, and rarely winged. The grapes are spherical and green with brown flecks that turn golden in favourable exposures. They are fairly thin-skinned with juicy neutral-tasting flesh that has a slightly acidulous quality.

24,000 hectares) but plantings have since fallen in favour of other vines. In 1996, Sylvaner accounted for just 7,420 hectares, divided between Rheinhessen, the Pfalz, Franconia (where the grapes perform best), the Nahe, Baden and Württemberg. In Switzerland, vineyardists in the Valais specialise in a wine known as Johannisberg which combines the characteristic acidity of Sylvaner with an elegant roundness. In Italian-speaking Switzerland, some Sylvaner vines are trellised against the walls. Elsewhere, there are plantings of Sylvaner in Italy, Luxembourg,

Also known as…

In Switzerland, Sylvaner is known as Gros Rhin in Geneva, Gros Riesling or Plant du Rhin in the Vaud and Johannisberg or Grande Arvine in the Valais. Californian vineyardists call it Franken Riesling, Monterey Riesling or Sonoma Riesling. In Germany, Sylvaner is spelt Silvaner.

Hungary (around Lake Balaton), Slovenia and other eastern European countries. Across the Atlantic, California has some Sylvaner in Monterey County (where Sylvaner wines are marketed as Monterey Riesling). Sylvaner is also grown in Australia, New Zealand, South Africa and Argentina. In all, total plantings of Sylvaner worldwide are close to 12,000 hectares.

Taste

Sylvaner produces two styles of wine: simple, refreshing wines that are low in alcohol; and delicately floral wines (acacia and white flowers) punctuated by a lemony fragrance. For the best wines – usually from grapes grown on sandy, calcareous soils – a short maturation of just three years can encourage more complex mineral nuances. Sylvaner wines always retain a slightly acidic palate.

Syrah

The precise origins of this great Rhône Valley grape remain a mystery. According to popular legend, it originated from the town of Schiraz in Iran and was brought back from the crusades by the Chevalier Stérimberg, who retired in 1224 to the hillside of Hermitage. Others maintain that Syrah was first introduced in France in the third century when Emperor Probus authorised the resumption of vine plantings in Gaul. A third hypothesis is that Syrah may be native to the Rhône Valley.

Vineyard profile

Syrah is characterised by relatively late bud burst and rather low fertility. However, attempts to increase yields tend to be counter-productive, producing wines of poorer quality with less aromatic potential. This grape variety is also sensitive to various pests and diseases and its shoots break easily in strong winds.

In France

Since 1960, Syrah cultivation in France has boomed, rising from 1,603 hectares in 1958 to 44,823 hectares in 1998. Not only does it form part of the blend of numerous AOC red wines, but it is also used to make single varietal red and rosé

wines in its own right. The cradle of Syrah cultivation is the northern valley of the Rhône in the neighbouring appellations of Côte-Rôtie, Cornas, Hermitage, Crozes-Hermitage and St-Joseph. These magnificent vineyards on sheer slopes rising impressively above the Rhône do, however, create difficult conditions for the local *vignerons*. Over the centuries, men have had to shape the landscape, creating terraces held up by dry-stone walls called *cheys*. The only machine that can be used here is a winch to lift and lower the baskets at harvest time. Syrah vines attached to stakes, either individually as in Cornas or two at a time as in St-Joseph, reveal different characteristics depending on the

terroir. On the Côte-Rôtie, for instance, Côte Blonde wines are soft and elegant, while those produced on the Côte Brune have a more robust quality.

Syrah has been planted extensively further to the south, where it once accounted for small-scale plantings in certain parts of the Châteauneuf-du-Pape appellation. In the first half of the 20th century Syrah was, in fact, only present in the Côtes-du-Rhône AOC. Today, thanks to a considerable programme of expansion, Syrah is grown in the following southern AOCs: Costières-de-Nîmes, Coteaux-du-Languedoc, Faugères, St-Chinian, Corbières, Minervois and even Côtes-du-Roussillon. Syrah vines have also been planted for the production of Vins de Pays d'Oc.

Around the world

Now popular in many winegrowing countries, Syrah (known locally as Shiraz) was introduced to Australian

Left: The Côte-Rotie produces elegant wines from Syrah grown on Gneiss soils. Above: The Hermitage hillside combines an ideal south-facing aspect with a *terroir* of granitic arènes.

Only the most
basic machinery
can be used on
the steeply
sloping vineyards
of Hermitage.

Opposite: Syrah,
known locally as
Shiraz, is the
leading red grape
variety in
Australia. The
wines it produces
in the Barossa
and Hunter
Valleys are
particularly well
respected.

Hermitage

This celebrated wine is a delightful garnet-red in youth with a subtly spicy bouquet of red berries. With age Hermitage acquires floral nuances of violets combined with the delicious aromas of cooked fruits (plums) and the scent of undergrowth. The palate has undeniably powerful tannic structure, becoming much silkier after five years of age. Depending on the vintage and the *terroir*, Hermitage wines are capable of up to ten years of ageing.

vineyards in New South Wales and South Australia in the 19th century. It became associated with a variety of styles, ranging from ordinary table wines produced from unrestricted yields to rich wines with excellent ageing potential; Grange, developed by Penfolds in their cellars in Nuriootpa in the Barossa Valley, and on the Magill Estate around Adelaide, is the best-known example of this. This idea for this famous wine was conceived in the 1950s, when the then technical director of the company, Max Schubert, returned from the Médoc with an ambition to make a great wine for laying down. Vinified according to Bordeaux methods and aged in wood, Grange was a resounding success and became Penfold's flagship wine. Syrah is also cultivated in

Identifying the grape variety

Syrah has a felty white growing tip with a crimson border. The leaves are orbicular with a bullate, contorted, often wavy appearance and five moderately defined lobes. The petiolar sinus is lyre-shaped and more or less closed, and the underside of the blade is pubescent with downy tufts. In the autumn, the leaves become red around the edges. The grape bunches of Syrahare cylindrical and sometimes winged, forming a compact mass of small, blue-black ovoid grapes with a thin, but fairly tough skin, thickly coated with bloom. The flesh is succulent with a pleasant taste.

Also known as...

There are several ways of spelling Syrah, including Sirah, Syra and even Schiras. On the Côte-Rôtie, it is sometimes called Serine. In Australia, it is known by the names of Shiraz and Hermitage after the famous French vineyard.

South Africa with promising results; also in Argentina, Mexico and California (in Mendocino and Sonoma). In Europe, Syrah is popular in Italy and Switzerland, where it can produce some fine wines in the Valais. Plantings of Syrah worldwide total some 65,000 hectares.

Colour and Taste

Syrah wines are deeply coloured and rich in tannins. Cornas, for instance, is so dark in colour that it is known as *vin noir* (black wine). The bouquet is characterised by a delicious aroma of violets that develops into peppery or smoky notes depending on the *terroir*. Syrah vinified alone gives wines of moderate ageing ability, such as Crozes-Hermitage and some St-Joseph, and crus requiring long-term cellaring, such as Hermitage, Côte-Rôtie and Cornas. Usually aged in wood, these wines need a certain amount of time to achieve a well-balanced structure and smooth tannic framework.

Ugni blanc

Of Italian origin, Ugni Blanc remains the most widely cultivated white grape variety in France. More usually associated with the production of Cognac and Armagnac, it is also used to produce many AOC wines and *vins de pays*.

The poet Frédéric Mistral said of the wines of Cassis: 'Bees do not make sweeter honey than this limpid jewel of our fragrant hillsides scented with rosemary, heather and myrtle'.

Vineyard profile

Ugni Blanc is a vigorous variety and is resistant to spring frosts, thanks to late bud burst. It nevertheless remains sensitive to winter frosts, such as the severe frosts of 1956 that wreaked havoc in the Languedoc. When planted ungrafted in sandy coastal vineyards, Ugni Blanc also attracts eelworms. It has the advantage of offering good resistance to powdery mildew and grey rot, which is why it has replaced Folle Blanche in the Charente. Ugni Blanc suits all forms of pruning, provided the fragile shoots that easily become detached from the old canes are protected from the wind.

In the Midi, Ugni Blanc produces some 100–150 hectolitres per hectare of wine with a satisfactory alcohol content (11-12 per cent abv). In the Charente, which represents the northern limit of cultivation for this late-maturing variety, productivity remains high but alcohol content is significantly lower (7–9 per cent abv). Ugni Blanc grapes are too small to be suitable as table grapes but they can be eaten as raisins as they dry out well during the winter.

In France

From 1958 to 1983, Ugni Blanc was the most widely propagated vine in French nurseries, with sales reaching a peak in 1982 when vineyards in Cognac were expanding. Plantings of Ugni Blanc have decreased slightly since then and now account for 94,000 hectares. Despite significant uprooting, Ugni Blanc plantings remain concentrated in the Charente and in Charente-Maritime (more than 77,330 hectares) where it produces white wines destined for distillation and blending as Cognac. The second most important region for Ugni Blanc is Armagnac, no less famous for its *eaux-de-vie*.

Ugni Blanc is not, however, exclusively used for distillation. In the Gironde, though clearly in

Among the many
varieties of
Trebbiano that
are cultivated in
Italy, the earliest
ripening is
Trebbiano Toscano
(around San
Gimignano in
Tuscany).

Cassis

Famous worldwide, Cassis white wine is traditionally based mainly on the Ugni Blanc grape, with the varieties of Marsanne and Clairette becoming increasingly important in its makeup. These pale, straw-coloured wines are discreet on the nose with delicate, underlying aromas of citrus, quince and lemon, and a suggestion of pine resin. The palate is fresh, rounded and long.

decline, it is an authorised white grape variety in the appellations of Bordeaux, Bordeaux Supérieur, Entre-Deux-Mers and Ste-Foy-Bordeaux. It is more significant in Provence, especially in the areas of Bandol, Bellet, Cassis, Côtes-de-Provence, Palette and the Coteaux-d'Aix-en-Provence. In Cassis, Ugni Blanc accounts for around 45 per cent of the white grape vines planted, although it is likely to be overtaken by Marsanne and Clairette. Ugny Blanc is still widely cultivated in the Languedoc to produce various wines known as Vins de Pays des Sables du Golfe du Lion, together with table wines. Corsica also grows some Ugni Blanc for the production of Vins de Corse and Ajaccio.

Identifying the grape variety

Ugni Blanc has a felty white growing tip with a crimson border. The leaves are large, thick and orbicular with a contorted appearance and five lobes. The surface of the blade is coarsely bullate and the underside is downy. The petiolar sinus is lyre-shaped and more or less closed. The grape bunches are very large, long and winged, packed with spherical, golden-yellow grapes that turn various shades of amber in favourable situations, finishing pink and even coppery-red on dry slopes in full sun. The skin is thin but tough, and the berries are fleshy and juicy.

Around the world

Altogether, plantings of Ugni Blanc worldwide total 190,000 hectares, with Italy being the second largest producer of all after France (58,480 hectares). Trebbiano Toscano (the local name for Ugni Blanc) plays a part in most of the white Italian appellation wines. Elsewhere in Europe, Ugni Blanc is cultivated in Bulgaria, Romania, Russia, Greece and Portugal (in the Ribatejo and in the south). In the New World, many countries use Ugni Blanc exclusively for distillation, as in Mexico and California (in the San Joaquin Valley). Brazil, Uruguay, South Africa and Australia also grow Ugni Blanc.

Also known as...

Ugni Blanc is known by the name of Clairette à Grains Ronds or Clairette Ronde in Provence and sometimes Roussan in Bellet. In the Charente it was traditionally known as St-Emilion until this was forbidden by law in 1988. The Italian name for Ugni Blanc is Trebbiano, and this is thought to have originated from an ancient village in Luni, Etruria (near the mouth of the river Magra in the Gulf of La Spezia). In the Roman hills it is called Procanico or Passarena. In Portugal, Ugni Blanc is known as Talia or Branquinha in the Ribatejo, and Douradinha in the Vinhos Verdes.

Taste

In northern regions, such as Cognac, Ugni Blanc produces wines that are high in acidity but low in aroma and these are ideal for distillation. (Rich wines with too much flavour would produce excessively strong *eaux-de-vie*, which would lose their balance with age.) In Mediterranean regions, on the other hand, Ugni Blanc yields rather neutral-tasting wines with low acidity. These are blended with Clairette, Grenache Blanc or Sauvignon Blanc, which add more complex aromas and structure.

Vermentino

Fashionable in the south of France, Vermentino is cultivated mainly in Provence, Corsica, Liguria and Sardinia, and is proving increasingly popular in Languedoc-Roussillon as well.

Bellet

Bellet wines are pale yellow in colour with green reflections and have an agreeable citrussy bouquet (lemons, oranges, grapefruit) bolstered by notes of lime blossom. The palate is a harmony of roundness and freshness.

Vineyard profile

Vermentino is a vigorous grape variety with good resistance to grey rot, but low resistance to powdery mildew. Although used principally for winemaking, the grapes may be eaten fresh or dried.

In France

Thanks to new plantings in the Midi, Vermentino has now established a presence in France where it accounts for 2,620 hectares. In Corsica, Vermentino is known locally as Vermentinu or Malvoisi and adds floral and citrus aromas to the white wines of Ajaccio and Patrimonio. In Ajaccio, it is sometimes blended with Ugni Blanc, Grenache and Cinsaut, while in Patrimonio it is often vinified alone. In Provence, the tiny vineyard of Bellet north of Nice produces limited quantities of a wine that is the embodiment of Ugni Blanc (known locally as Rolle). While in other Provençal appellations, white wine production is far outweighed by red, here in Bellet they account for a reasonable 30 per cent of output (equal to that of rosé wines). However, there is

Identifying the grape variety

Vermentino has a felty white growing tip with a crimson border. The leaves are bluish-green, orbicular and contorted with a delicately bullate appearance and five sharply defined lobes. The petiolar sinus is lyre-shaped and closed, and the underside of the blade is downy. The grape bunches are truncate and quite large with a well-developed wing. The grapes are white, turning pink when fully ripe.

continuing debate as to whether or not Rolle is the same vine as Vermentino, despite their similar ampelographical characteristics. Vermentino also contributes to other white Provençal wines, except those from Cassis and Bandol. Though plantings remain limited, Vermentino continues to make progress in the vineyards of Languedoc-Roussillon, especially in the Coteaux-du-Languedoc and the Costières-de-Nîmes, as in the Côtes-du-Roussillon.

Around the world

In Italy, Vermentino is among the vines planted in several DOCs, including Cinqueterre in Liguria (see picture right) and Vermentino di Gallura in Sardinia. Portugal also grows Vermentino in Madeira. Plantings worldwide total some 7,000 hectares.

Also known as...

Vermentino is also known by a variety of names worldwide such as: Rolle in Bellet, Provence; Vermentinu in Corsica and Sardinia; Malvoisie de Corse or Malvoisie à Gros Grains in the Var; and Pigato in Liguria.

Taste

Vermentino wines are pale-coloured and aromatic with a delightful bouquet of flowers, fruit and aniseed, and a rounded, supple palate. They are ready for drinking one year after vinification, but can be left for two or three years with no loss of quality.

Viognier

Nobody knows the precise origins of this white grape variety, established for centuries on the terraced vineyards of Condrieu and Ampuis on the right bank of the Rhône. Legend has it that Viognier vines were first introduced by the Emperor Probus from Smirnium in Croatia, known locally as Vulgava Bijela, and are cultivated particularly on the island of Vis in Dalmatia. Ampelographers these days favour the opinion that Viognier is of local origin, derived from ancient wild vines that were cultivated and improved by the Allobroges tribe, who settled in the Rhône Valley.

Condrieu and Château-Grillet

Perfectly ripe Viognier grapes grown on these steep granitic terraces produce a range of opulent, rounded, well-balanced wines in varying shades of gold. Their complex bouquet presents sustained aromas of fruit (apricots and peaches) and white flowers, plus additional notes of honey and toast in very ripe vintages. Condrieu wines tend to age well.

Vineyard profile

Viognier is a hardy grape variety giving low yields – around 20 hectolitres per hectare in Condrieu. It requires long-pruning to yield a sufficient crop and only exceeds 30 hectolitres per hectare in good years. Viognier is vulnerable to powdery mildew, but rarely to *coulure* and it is generally resistant to drought. To reach its full aromatic potential, Viognier needs to have plenty of warmth and carefully selected sites.

In France

In the early 1960s, Viognier plantings were limited to 30 hectares supplying the needs of the appellations of Condrieu, Château-Grillet and the Côte-Rôtie. *Vignerons* at the time showed relatively little interest in this low-yield vine that was difficult to cultivate. However, in the 1980s a renewed interest in the wines of

Identifying the grape variety

Viognier has a white, downy or almost felty growing tip with a crimson border. Young leaves are cobwebby with bronze patches. The mature blade is orbicular, bullate and contorted with five moderately defined lobes, an open U-shaped petiolar sinus and a downy underside. Grape bunches are truncate and sometimes winged, forming a compact mass of small spherical or slightly ovoid amber-white grapes, thick skinned, with delicately musky-tasting flesh.

the Rhône led to the spread of Viognier to many southern vineyards. There are now 2,620 hectares planted in France. While it is an authorised variety in the regional appellations of the Côtes-du-Rhône, it is mainly planted on the right bank of the northern Rhône between Vienne and Valence on steep vineyard terraces favoured by a sunny microclimate. Condrieu and Château-Grillet, for many years overshadowed by their more illustrious neighbour the Côte-Rôtie, benefited significantly from Viognier's international recognition in 1980. Thus the Condrieu vineyard grew – and now covers 101 hectares. Meanwhile, the exceptionally small vineyard of Château-Grillet, a *monopole* or single-ownership property

Also known as...

There are a few alternative spellings of Viognier, such as Vionnier, Petit Vionnier and Viognié.

belonging to the Neyret-Grachet family, actually reached 3.4 hectares. In fact, Viognier is more prevalent on the Côte Blonde than on the Côte Brune, which may seem surprising for a wine region specialising in red wines. However, up to 20 per cent of Viognier has always been authorised here to complement Syrah.

Around the world

Viognier was introduced into the United States at the end of the 1980s. Vineyardists in California, Virginia and Georgia were among the first to test the new vine, forming an association called The Viognier Guild with French *vignerons* from the Rhône Valley. Elsewhere, there are limited plantings of Viognier in Brazil (in the Garibaldi region) and South Australia (in Yalumba). It is also a recommended variety in various Portuguese vineyards ranging from the Minho to the Beiras, the Ribatejo and the Oeste, the Alentejo and the Algarve.

Taste

Vinified alone, Viognier produces premium quality white wines with aromas of apricots, peaches, white flowers, spices and honey; the palate is rounded and low in acid.

ALIGOTÉ
(23,000 hectares)

CABERNET FRANC
(45,000 hectares)

CABERNET-SAUVIGNON
(165,000 hectares)

CARIGNAN
(160,000 hectares)

CHARDONNAY
(130,000 hectares)

ALIGOTÉ	CABERNET FRANC	CABERNET-SAUVIGNON		CARIGNAN	CHARDONNAY	
Albania	Albania	Albania	Moldavia	Algeria	Argentina	South Africa
Azerbaijan	Argentina	Argentina	Morocco	Argentina	Australia	Spain
Bulgaria	Australia	Australia	New Zealand	Australia	Austria	Switzerland
Canada	Brazil	Austria	Peru	Brazil	Bulgaria	Tunisia
France	Canada	Bosnia-Herzegovina	Romania	Chile	Canada	Ukraine
Georgia	Chile	Brazil	Russia	China	Chile	USA
Kazakhstan	China	Bulgaria	Slovakia	Cyprus	China	_CALIFORNIA_
Kirghizistan	Cyprus	Canada	Slovenia	Dominican	Colombia	_OREGON_
Moldavia	France	Chile	South Africa	Republic	Cyprus	_WASHINGTON_
Romania	Greece	China	Spain	France	France	_NEW YORK_
Russia	Hungary	Colombia	Thailand	India	Georgia	_VIRGINIA_
South Korea	India	Croatia	Tunisia	Israel	Germany	_NEW JERSEY_
Tanzania	Italy	Cyprus	Ukraine	Italy	Greece	_TEXAS_
Ukraine	Japan	France	USA	Mexico	Hungary	
	Morocco	Georgia	_CALIFORNIA_	Morocco	India	United Kingdom
	New Zealand	Germany	_WASHINGTON_	Peru	Israel	Uruguay
	Peru	Greece	_NEW YORK_	South Africa	Italy	
	South Africa	Hungary	_VIRGINIA_	Spain	Japan	
	Spain	India	_GEORGIA_	Tunisia	Kenya	
	Tanzania	Israel	_TEXAS_	USA	Kirghizistan	
	Tunisia	Italy	Uruguay	_CALIFORNIA_	Lichtenstein	
	USA	Japan	Venezuela	Uruguay	Luxembourg	
	CALIFORNIA	Kazakhstan	Vietnam		Moldavia	
	WASHINGTON	Lebanon			New Zealand	
	NEW YORK	Mexico			Romania	
	VIRGINIA				Slovakia	
	GEORGIA					
	TEXAS					
	Uruguay					

CHASSELAS	**CHENIN**	**CINSAUT**	**CLAIRETTE**	**COLOMBARD**	**GAMAY**	**GEWÜRZTRAMINER**
(35,000 hectares)	*(53,000 hectares)*	*(45,000 hectares)*	*(12,000 hectares)*	*(43,000 hectares)*	*(40,000 hectares)*	*(8,000 hectares)*

CHASSELAS	CHENIN	CINSAUT	CLAIRETTE	COLOMBARD	GAMAY	GEWÜRZTRAMINER
Byelorussia	Argentina	Algeria	Algeria	Australia	Bosnia-Herzegovina	Argentina
France	Australia	Argentina	Australia	France	Brazil	Austria
Germany	Bolivia	Brazil	France	India	Bulgaria	Bulgaria
Hungary	Canada	Bulgaria	Israel	Israel	Canada	Canada
New Zealand	Chile	Chile	Morocco	Kenya	Croatia	Chile
Switzerland	China	Cyprus	Romania	Mexico	France	Croatia
Uzbekistan	France	France	Russia	South Africa	India	France
	India	Israel	South Africa	Thailand	Israel	Germany
	Israel	Italy	Tunisia	USA	Luxembourg	Hungary
	Kenya	Morocco	Turkey	*CALIFORNIA*	Moldavia	Israel
	Mexico	South Africa		*TEXAS*	South Africa	Italy
	New Zealand	Thailand		Uruguay	Switzerland	Luxembourg
	Peru	Tunisia			Thailand	Moldavia
	South Africa	USA			Turkey	New Zealand
	Tanzania	*CALIFORNIA*			USA	Romania
	Thailand				*CALIFORNIA*	Russia
	USA				Vietnam	Slovakia
	CALIFORNIA				Former Yugoslavia	Slovenia
	WASHINGTON					South Africa
	TEXAS					Switzerland
	Uruguay					Tanzania
						Ukraine
						USA
						CALIFORNIA
						OREGON
						WASHINGTON
						NEW YORK
						VIRGINIA
						TEXAS
						Uruguay

GRENACHE (240,000 hectares)	**MARSANNE** (2,000 hectares)	**MAUZAC** (3,350 hectares)	**MELON** (14,000 hectares)	**MERLOT** (200,000 hectares)		**MONDEUSE** (250 hectares)
Algeria	Australia	France	Argentina	Albania	Switzerland	Australia
Argentina	France		France	Argentina	Thailand	France
Australia	Italy		USA	Australia	Tunisia	
Brazil	Switzerland		*CALIFORNIA*	Bolivia	USA	
Cyprus				Brazil	*CALIFORNIA*	
Dominican				Bulgaria	*WASHINGTON*	
Republic				Canada	*NEW YORK*	
France				Chile	*VIRGINIA*	
Israel				China	*TEXAS*	
Italy				Colombia	Uruguay	
Mexico				Croatia	Venezuela	
Morocco				Cyprus	Former	
Peru				France	Yugoslavia	
South Africa				Hungary		
Spain				Israel		
Tanzania				Italy		
Thailand				Japan		
Tunisia				Lebanon		
USA				Mexico		
CALIFORNIA				Moldavia		
WASHINGTON				New Zealand		
				Romania		
				Russia		
				Slovenia		
				South Africa		

N O P

MOURVÈDRE (85,000 hectares)	**MUSCADELLE** (5,000 hectares)	**MUSCAT BLANC** (45,000 hectares)	**MUSCAT OTTONEL** (2,000 hectares)	**NÉGRETTE** (1,400 hectares)	**ONDENC** (300 hectares)	**PETIT MANSENG** (1,570 hectares)

Australia	Australia	Albania	Australia	France	Australia	France
Azerbaijan	France	Argentina	Austria	USA *CALIFORNIA*	France	Uruguay
Cyprus	Russia	Australia	Bulgaria			
France	USA *CALIFORNIA*	Austria	Canada			
Spain		Brazil	Croatia			
Tunisia		Bulgaria	France			
Ukraine		Cyprus	Hungary			
USA *CALIFORNIA*		France	Moldavia			
Uzbekistan		Germany	Romania			
Venezuela		Greece	Slovenia			
		Hungary	South Africa			
		Portugal	Switzerland			
		Romania	Uruguay			
		Russia	Former Yugoslavia			
		Slovenia				
		South Africa				
		Spain				
		Turkey				
		USA *CALIFORNIA* *TEXAS*				
		Uruguay				
		Former Yugoslavia				
		Zambia				
		Zimbabwe				

PINOT NOIR
(60,000 hectares)

Pinot Noir		Poulsard	Riesling		Roussanne	Sauvignon
Argentina	Portugal	France	Albania	South Korea	Australia	Albania
Australia	Romania		Argentina	Spain	France	Argentina
Austria	Russia		Australia	Switzerland	USA	Australia
Azerbaijan	Slovakia		Austria	USA	*CALIFORNIA*	Austria
Belgium	Slovenia		Bolivia	*CALIFORNIA*		Bolivia
Brazil	South Africa		Brazil	*OREGON*		Brazil
Bulgaria	Switzerland		Bulgaria	*WASHINGTON*		Bulgaria
Canada	Tadzhikistan		Canada	*NEW YORK*		Canada
Czech Republic	Tunisia		Chile	*VIRGINIA*		Chile
Chile	Turkey		China	*NEW JERSEY*		China
Colombia	USA		Croatia	*GEORGIA*		Colombia
Croatia	*CALIFORNIA*		Cyprus	*TEXAS*		Croatia
France	*OREGON*		Czech Republic	United Kingdom		Cyprus
Georgia	*WASHINGTON*		France	Thailand		Czech Republic
Germany	*NEW YORK*		Germany	Turkmenistan		France
India	*VIRGINIA*		Hungary	Ukraine		Germany
Israel	United Kingdom		Israel	Venezuela		Hungary
Italy	Uruguay		Japan			India
Japan	Former		Luxembourg			Israel
Kazakhstan	Yugoslavia		Mexico			Italy
Kirghizistan			Moldavia			Kenya
Laos			New Zealand			Macedonia
Lichtenstein			Netherlands			Mexico
Luxembourg			Peru			Moldavia
Moldavia			Russia			New Zealand
New Zealand			Slovakia			Peru

POULSARD
(300 hectares)

R RIESLING
(60,000 hectares)

ROUSSANNE
(1,000 hectares)

S SAUVIGNON
(45,000 hectares)

158

SÉMILLON	**SYLVANER**	**SYRAH**	**UGNI BLANC**	**VERMENTINO**	**VIOGNIER**
(34,000 hectares)	*(12,000 hectares)*	*(65,000 hectares)*	*(190,000 hectares)*	*(7,000 hectares)*	*(3,000 hectares)*

	SÉMILLON	**SYLVANER**	**SYRAH**	**UGNI BLANC**	**VERMENTINO**	**VIOGNIER**
Romania	Argentina	Argentina	Argentina	Algeria	France	Brazil
Russia	Australia	Australia	Australia	Argentina	Italy	Chile
Slovakia	Bolivia	Austria	Brazil	Australia		France
Slovenia	Brazil	Czech Republic	Chile	Bulgaria		Portugal
South Africa	Chile	Chile	China	China		USA
Spain	China	Croatia	Colombia	Cyprus		*CALIFORNIA*
Switzerland	Croatia	France	Cyprus	France		*GEORGIA*
USA	Cyprus	Germany	France	Greece		
CALIFORNIA	France	Hungary	India	India		Uruguay
OREGON	Hungary	Italy	Mexico	Israel		
WASHINGTON	India	Luxembourg	Morocco	Italy		
NEW YORK	Israel	Moldavia	New Zealand	Mexico		
VIRGINIA	Japan	Nigeria	Thailand	Morocco		
GEORGIA	Macedonia	New Zealand	Tunisia	Peru		
TEXAS	Mexico	Russia	USA	Romania		
Thailand	New Zealand	Slovakia	*CALIFORNIA*	South Africa		
Ukraine	Peru	Slovenia	Uruguay	USA		
Uruguay	Russia	South Korea	Venezuela	*CALIFORNIA*		
Venezuela	South Africa	Switzerland		*TEXAS*		
Former	Switzerland	Turkey		Thailand		
Yugoslavia	USA			Tunisia		
	CALIFORNIA			Uruguay		
	WASHINGTON			Vietnam		
	TEXAS					
	Turkey					
	Ukraine					
	Uruguay					
	Venezuela					
	Former					
	Yugoslavia					

Acknowledgements

Charlus : 4.

D.R. : 33, 34 (bottom).

P. Galet : 8, 11, 16 (centre), 17, 24, 25, 27, 28, 29, 30, 34 (top), 35, 154-159.

Hachette Photo Library: 6, 7, 9, 10, 17.

C. Sarramon : Front cover, 22 (top x 2), 26, 47 (bottom), 49, 60 (bottom), 79, 85, 120, 143 (top).

SCOPE

• *J.-L. Barde :* 16 (bottom left and right), 18, 19 (bottom x 2), 48, 70 (bottom), 86, 86, 87, 95, 99, 105 , 106, 108, 113, 115, 117, 121, 137, 138 (bottom), 139, 143 (bottom), 144, 148.

• *D. Dutay :* 145.

• *H. Friedrichsmeier :* 60 (top).

• *J. Guillard :* 2, 13, 20, 21, 22 (bottom), 39, 41, 51, 53 (top), 56, 59, 61, 63, 69, 70 (top), 71, 73, 74, 75, 77, 78, 81, 82, 83, 100, 101, 119 (bottom), 122, 123 (bottom), 125, 128, 131, 133 , 134, 135, 147, 151.

• *M. Guillard :* 40, 45, 57, 67, 138 (top).

• *N. Hautemanière :* 47 (top).

• *F. Jalain :* Back cover

• *S. Matthews :* 43, 53 (bottom), 90 (top), 94, 109, 123 (top).

• *F. Nussbaumer :* 127.

• *M. Plassart :* 89, 90 (bottom), 91, 119 (top).

• *N. Servian :* 19 (top).

Editorial Director: Catherine Montalbetti
Design: Graph'm/François Huertas
Ampelography plates illustrated by Ferdinand Dhoska
English Translation by: Florence Brutton
Copy edited by: Sue Morony

First published in Great Britain in 2002
by Cassell Illustrated,
a division of Octopus Publishing Group Limited
2-4 Heron Quays, London E14 4JP

English Translation © Octopus Publishing Group Ltd 2002
© Hachette Livre (Hachette Practique) 2001

Distributed in the United States of America by
Sterling Publishing Co., Inc.,
387 Park Avenue South, new York, NY 10016-8810

A CIP catalogue record for this book is available from the British Library.

ISBN 0 304 36409 6

Printed in Singapore

Cassell Illustrated
A Division of the Octopus Publishing Group Ltd
2–4 Heron Quays, London E14 4JP